FROM GUNS TO BINOCULARS
BY
G. H. (JOSH) SCOTT

William Memmory.
" Bain Meadow.
West Lane.
Haltham -
Horncastle. LN9 6JG.
Lincolnshire.

From Guns to Binoculars

by

G. H. (JOSH) SCOTT

With a Foreword by Sir Peter Scott, CBE, DSC

Line drawings by Lewis Todd

Providence Press

Acknowledgements
Where known copyright of photographs is acknowledged.

First published 1980 by Providence Press, Wardy Hill, Ely, Cambridgeshire.

ISBN   0-903803-06-2

Contents

TO CAROLYN

Foreword

The Fens first captured my imagination more than 50 years ago when I visited the Ouse Washes as a wildfowler, and my interest in them and their great assemblies of water birds has never waned.

Regular visits from Cambridge undergraduate days gave way to less regular visits when my home was in a lighthouse on the Wash. After the war there were visits to assess the possibilities of various wetlands as nature reserves and in 1967 the Wildfowl Trust acquired its first land holdings in the Ouse Washes near Welney.

The shepherd of those Washes was a fenman, wildfowler and naturalist who was the obvious choice as Warden of the new reserve.

I am delighted that he has recorded the experiences and adventures of his early life in this his first book. I also look forward to a sequel which I believe is planned, that will describe in greater detail the development of the Welney Wildfowl Refuge with its seasonal specialities—its winter wild swans, and huge flocks of wigeon, and its summer breeding birds, which include rarities like Black-tailed Godwit, Reeve, Black Tern, Little Ringed Plover and Garganey, among many other duck species and a profusion of nesting snipe.

As guardian of these treasures Josh Scott has made a host of friends among ornithological enthusiasts who will greatly enjoy this book. I am happy to be associated with it and to wish it every success.

Peter Scott

1. Early Days

Although I have always been known as a Norfolk 'bor' because I have lived most of my life in the Norfolk village of Welney, I was in fact born in the Cambridgeshire Parish of Littleport. At that time my parents lived in a small cottage only about 300 yards from the county boundary and much closer to Welney than to the town of Littleport. We lived there until I was seven and the only vivid memory I have of the cottage is of the quaint bedrooms, with lean-to ceilings, built almost entirely in the roof.

The cottage became too small for us as our family grew, so we moved down the road a little way on the Norfolk side of the boundary.

The main part of Welney village is on the west side of the Old Bedford river but our cottage was about a mile away on the east side of the New Bedford or Hundred Foot river, in the small hamlet of 'Suspension Bridge' named after the first bridge to be built over the Hundred Foot river. Between the rivers lie the Hundred Foot Washes which were created in the first half of the 17th century, when the rivers were dug under the supervision of the Dutch engineer, Cornelius Vermuyden. His idea was to create an area into which flood waters of the Ouse could be directed and stored for later discharge at Wellmore Lake Sluice, near Denver. These washes (usually now called the Ouse Washes) have always been of the greatest importance to me. On them I first learned to fish, to shoot, to catch plover, to punt gun and generally earn a livelihood as a shepherd, until I became Warden when the Wildfowl Trust established its Welney Refuge in 1967.

Prior to the erection of the suspension bridge in 1825, there was a ferry across the Hundred Foot river, the profits from which belonged to the Bedford Level Corporation which was, at that time, responsible for the maintenance of the main drainage rivers in the Fens. The bridge was built by the Revd. William Gale of Upwell, who was empowered under a lease from the Corporation 'to demand and take certain tolls for passing over the bridge.' It remained in use for just over 100 years and was not replaced until 1927. For a time my uncle was the collector of tolls and as a small boy I can remember being told to watch for approaching vehicles. As soon as one was in sight I ran down the steep bank to fetch him from the Crown or the Carpenter's Arms so that he could get to the bridge to collect the toll. He usually had plenty of time as vehicles could only travel very slowly on the poor gravel roads.

I think the tolls were 6d for a horse and cart, pony and trap or car, 2d for a motor cycle and 1d for a pedestrian or cyclist. Uncle gave me a ha'penny each time I fetched him from the pub. This I spent at Mrs. Jackson's shop, which was nearby. Usually I bought a stick of liquorice as there was not such a wide choice of sweets in those days and I thought this gave me the best value for money.

In its later years the bridge became insecure and the boards on the floor very loose and noisy when anything passed over them. The last cattle to cross before it was demolished were made to go singly. Although the old bridge has gone the name of our hamlet remains.

From the day that I started school until the day I finished, I hated every minute I spent within the confines of its four walls or within its playground. My first memories are of attending a small school close to the suspension bridge. When I was about ten years old it was closed because the building was said to be unsafe but it is still standing today and I think its closure was due to a shortage of teachers rather than for any other reason.

After that, all the children from Suspension Bridge went to Welney school. Each morning we were picked up by a 'bus, driven by its owner who was also our postman. The change pleased me more than any of the other children as I knew that from time to time the washes would be flooded and there would be no schooling for us. When freed from school in this way I usually spent most of the day helping my father with his stock or in watching other men at their work. Occasionally I joined other children and played with them on the high ground near the bridge. We watched intently when we saw a vehicle approaching as often the driver was not local and was therefore very surprised after crossing the bridge to be confronted with a flooded road. He was faced with either attempting to go through the water or a long detour through Hilgay and Downham Market and would almost always ask 'How deep is it?' before deciding what to do.

We would all quickly gather round and eagerly assure the driver that the water was only a few inches deep and that he should be able to get through. We knew full well that the road surface was very uneven and in some places the water would be at least 18 inches deep. Sometimes the vehicle got through but more often than not it became stuck in the middle and the driver would call for help. This was what we always hoped for as we got a few pennies for pushing him out.

In the summer it was easy as all we had to do was wade in and push but in the winter, when the water was icy cold, another strategy was used. Then I went to the village to fetch a man with a horse and at the same time to borrow my father's waders. I was an essential part of the team as the horseman did not have any waders. He rode the horse and I waded in to fix the chain to the vehicle, while the driver remained stranded in the cab. Usually I was given a shilling or two for my trouble while the horseman received ten shillings.

Between the ages of seven and fourteen I spent most of my winter evenings with other boys, on or near the bridge, lounging around and passing the time as best we could. Some of the older ones who were working could afford to buy cigarettes and from time to time would send one of the younger ones to buy a packet at the Carpenter's Arms. They could buy ten Woodbines or ten Park Drive for 4d or ten Players for 6d (2½p).

If there were six lads they would each give a penny and while the cigarettes were being fetched, each had a guess at the number of the card in the packet. The one whose guess was nearest had the packet but the boy who had run the errand got nothing, not even the card or a puff from a cigarette.

One particular evening I was on the bridge when 6d was collected and I was sent for the cigarettes. Unknown to me, during the day a heap of sugar beet had been put on the bank and as I ran down it in the darkness I tumbled over the beet and landed on the gravel road at the bottom.

I shrieked out in agony as I had hurt my leg so badly that I was unable to walk. The lads managed to carry me home and when I got into the lamp-lit room I saw that there was a large piece of sharp gravel stuck firmly into my knee. It had gone in about three-quarters of an inch and when removed left a gaping hole surrounded by lacerated flesh. After my mother had washed it thoroughly my father trimmed the fragments of skin with his cut-throat razor. I felt nothing of this as my knee was numb but when he poured undiluted iodine over it I instantly recovered my feelings. My mother said afterwards she thought I was going to scream the house down when the iodine was applied.

I expect the reason why my parents did not take me to the doctor was simply that they could not afford to do so. Instead, they took me to see the Welney rector's daughter, who was a qualified nurse and happened to be home at the time. After she had dressed the wound she said that I should have a complete rest and keep off my legs for a few days. My great uncle, old Will Kent, and great aunt who lived in a little cottage in the washes suggested that I should stay with them while my leg healed.

3

It was during this enforced stay with them that I got my first insight into the home life of a professional wildfowler. As it was autumn there was a great amount going on and when old Will arrived home he would talk about how successful, or otherwise, his day had been. Although at that time I did not really understand all the problems which beset a wildfowler, I loved to listen to him telling my aunt how good the plover catching had been, or how the duck were flighting or about the troubles he had with the cattle.

Sometimes he came home soaking after a day spent cleaning out dykes or in cutting osiers for the local basket maker. A few times I watched him preparing his punt gun before setting off into the flooded washes. He was so patient in stalking the duck or geese that I got tired of watching and waiting for the report of the gun to echo across the water. I longed to go with him and hoped that one day he would teach me the art of punt gunning but he never did.

It was while living with old Will that I had my first pair of wellington boots. They were given to me by my cousin who only parted with them because, in his opinion, they were absolutely worn out. However, I thought they would be useful for me and so with more enthusiasm than skill, I set to work to make them watertight.

I managed to get a tube of rubber solution and a piece of sandpaper but as I could not afford to buy any patches I cut some pieces from an old bicycle tube to use instead. There were thirteen holes and by the time I had finished there seemed to be more tube than original boot. When all the patches were dry I went along to the washes and gave the boots a thorough testing by walking up and down several dykes. They passed with flying colours and I went proudly back to tell my great aunt.

The first time I used them after that was when I had gone back to live at home. A heavy fall of snow provided the chance that I so eagerly awaited. As I put my wellingtons on that morning I felt so pleased that for the first time in my life I should be able to walk in the deep snow without getting my feet wet. When I found that one foot was getting very cold I could have cried as I thought that one boot was, in spite of all my efforts, still not watertight.

I was so distressed that I took it off only to find that it was perfectly dry and that my foot was just cold. Without realising what I was doing I foolishly put my stockinged foot on the snow so that when I put my boot on again I really had got a wet foot. As I grew older, I helped father with his smallholding and also worked for other farmers and many a time I was thankful that I had my boots to wear.

The new bridge was built when I was nine years old. Its construction brought work to the area at a period when farming was beginning to plunge into a state of depression. The Norfolk County Council hired as many horses and carts as could be spared by local farmers. They were needed for carting vast quantities of silt which was used for improving the existing narrow road from toll corner, and to build up the approaches to the new bridge. The silt was obtained from the banks of the Hundred Foot river and was brought down to the road on a light railway which had been put down especially for this purpose.

Father was anxious to earn some money and hired out his horse and cart. Unfortunately, the horse was stabled about a mile from where we lived and had to be fetched from there each morning and returned again at night. Father, who was always up very early to tend his stock, gave the horse his feed or 'bait' as we called it. Before he came home to breakfast he put the harness on and put the horse into the cart. It was my task to walk down to the farm and fetch the horse and cart so that it was ready to start work at the bridge at 8 o'clock. When I came out of school I collected it again and took it back to the farm.

The common practice of the farm men was to ride on the horse, sitting sideways with their feet resting on the shafts. I was too small to do this and used to have a rather precarious ride perched astride between the collar and saddle. This was not a riding saddle but an essential part of the cart horse's harness. The upper part of the wood had a groove into which fitted the back chain which supported the shafts. Because the weight of the cart was thus transferred to the horse's back, the under part of the saddle was well padded with a cushion of wheat straw. The collar was the part of the harness against which the horse pushed while in the cart, or any other implement. It was also padded but for this, longer rye straw was preferred. Most of the harness was made locally at Wright's of Littleport.

The haymaking season provided schoolboys with a chance to earn a few pennies. Usually this was during the holidays but if I was needed during the term my father kept me away from school.

My employer was a Manea farmer who kept a large number of horses to use in growing vegetable crops on his fenland farm. He owned an extensive area of land in the washes, much of which is now owned by the Wildfowl Trust. Each year he made about 150 acres of hay for feeding to his horses in the winter.

During haymaking the working horses were confined to a narrow drove on the washes so that they were easy to catch by the horse-keepers who cycled over from Manea each day. They arrived very early in the morning so that the horses were able to finish eating their bait of oats and chaff half an hour or more before they had to be harnessed up, ready to start work when the day men got there.

All the hay was cut with horse-drawn haycutters. As it was very hard work the horses were not used for the whole day. After the horse-keeper had finished his lunch, or 'dockey' as we called it, at 11 o'clock, a fresh pair would be used. If cutting was to continue long into the afternoon, a third pair would be put on or perhaps the first pair would be used again. As each haycutter could only cut four to five acres a day, two machines were used so that as much of the hay as possible could be made during a spell of fine weather.

As soon as some of the swaths of grass had begun to dry, the day men began to turn them by hand although sometimes a horse-drawn tedder was used. After the hay had dried sufficiently it was raked into rows with a horse-rake and then collected by the men into small heaps or cocks. Once in the cocks it was protected to some extent from rain but if it did get wet it was spread out to dry before being heaped up again. Haymaking in this way required a large number of workers. It was a slow process but no effort was spared to ensure that all the hay was of high quality, free from mould and over-heated patches. Top quality was essential to keep the working horses healthy and fit.

When carting started, boys were needed for driving the horses and wagons on their long journeys between the washes and the Manea farmyard. The younger lads up to the age of about eleven were not considered safe on the public roads but drove the horses the mile or so from the hayfields to the road near the bridge. There they met the older boys who had brought the empty wagons back from Manea.

The loaded carts were taken the long way round by Tipsend as the huge loads of loose hay, although securely tied down with wagon rope, were not secure enough for the rough droves along which the empty carts trundled on the return journey.

Throughout haymaking the air was full of the scent of newly mown hay and the particular smell of meadowsweet which was a common weed on the washes.

In the summer evenings I sometimes went for a swim at Bank Farm where there was a small hole normally well filled with water from the Hundred Foot river. It was fed by a siphon which started to operate when the tide was high enough to prime it. At times, when tides were low, it had to be primed with a pump. All the tanks used for water for the pigs, together with the troughs in the horse and cattle yards, were filled from the siphon, as was the hole in which we swam.

One evening when the level was low and the water rather muddy, my friend Kit Malkin (whose full name was Harold Kitchener) suggested that we should swim in the river. It seemed a good idea so we ran across the road, over the bank and I dived in and swam until I was exhausted, then climbed out on to the bank for a rest.

Meanwhile Kit, who could not swim, was enjoying himself in the water, keeping his feet on the bottom while he 'dog-paddled' along. Unfortunately, he got out of his depth and was taken out further by the tide. I heard him call and saw him go down twice before I reached him and took hold of his hands. Somehow we reached the bank, struggled out and more or less collapsed on the grass. I was terribly frightened that he would drown but he was terrified at the prospect of having to go home and tell his father what had happened.

Eventually it grew dark and we had to go and face the music but of course his parents were so relieved that he was alive that they did not scold him. His father, Saul Malkin, who was landlord at The Crown said that his pub was open to me at any time. It was after this that I started to play darts although legally I was still too young to go into a public house. For the time he remained landlord, Kit's father would always lend me money for cigarettes or drinks and never forgot his gratitude for my having rescued Kit from the river.

In my early schooldays my father had a small piece of land which he shared with his nephew. The profits from the crops supplemented the rather meagre earnings which he obtained from shepherding on the washes in the summer and wildfowling in the winter.

As the number of mouths which had to be fed increased, he decided to give up this land. Instead, with a small dairy herd, he started a retail milk round. Much of the work of tending the cows fell to me. Before going to school the cowshed had to be cleaned out and littered with fresh dry straw in readiness for when the herd came in for the afternoon milking. In the winter, mangolds had to be scraped clean, sliced and mixed with chaff for the evening and following morning feeds. Throughout the year all the concrete had to be washed and brushed down. For this, water had to be carried in buckets on a yolk from the Hundred Foot river. This entailed crossing the road and climbing up and over the bank to reach the water.

When I was eleven years old father had six cows and he began to teach me to milk the easier, quieter ones. There were no milking machines so I had to sit on a three-legged stool and squeeze the teats as best I could with my small hands. At first the muscles in my hands and arms ached after each milking but I soon acquired a certain amount of skill. By the age of twelve I was often left to milk all the cows myself. When father was particularly busy with his other work I was sometimes lucky enough to be kept away from school to look after the cows.

The land which father gave up was taken over by his nephew, who I was sometimes sent to help. I particularly remember having to fetch a horse and cart which a friend of his, who lived near Shippea Hill station, let him borrow for muck carting. It was the practice in those days to cart the litter from the cattle yards during the spring or early summer and put it into a heap on a wheat field. There it was left to rot down until the corn had been harvested, when it could be carted out into small heaps. It was then spread by hand before being ploughed in prior to planting potatoes.

I cycled to Shippea Hill, putting my bicycle into the cart for the return journey. Fenland horses were trained to be driven with a single line when at work on the land but by law a double rein had to be used for driving on a public road.

I was only just big enough to see over the front of the cart and undertook the journey with considerable apprehension. My route was along the Mildenhall road, over Littleport bridge on the A10, until I had to turn off for Welney at the Crown corner in Littleport. A haulage contractor in the town operated a number of steam lorries and, as the horse was rather nervous of them, I was always afraid that one would come along just as I was turning the corner. I was always very relieved to be heading for home along the Welney road. When muck carting was finished, it fell to me to return the horse and cart to its owner.

As I grew older, I started helping with the milk round and my absences from school became more frequent. For the round father used a bicycle with a sidecar, on which stood a 10-gallon and a 2-gallon churn. He went from house to house measuring out the amount of milk asked for with a half-pint measure which hung on the inside of one of the churns. I did the milk round from time to time until one of my sisters was old enough to take over.

When my brothers and sisters began to help with the cows and milk round, I helped various small farmers when they needed extra labour for threshing, taking up potatoes or during the corn harvesting. My parents badly needed the money which I could earn so that I was often sent to work rather than to school.

I cannot remember how many times father appeared before the Magistrate at Downham Market because of summonses arising from my absence from school but the last occasion I can recall quite clearly.

I was thirteen and doing a day's threshing for Freddie Cross who had a smallholding not far from where we lived. A set of threshing tackle consisting of a portable engine, an old drum and a jack straw had been hired for the day. Freddie, knowing that I was accustomed to work and strong for my age, told me that if I worked on a corn stack, which was one of the hardest jobs, he would give me a man's pay for the day. I accepted his offer.

Father had once again received a summons to appear at Downham Market Magistrates' Court. As usual, he cycled to Hilgay station and took his bicycle on the train so that he could cycle up to the Police Station. By the time he returned, threshing was over as there was only a small stack to do.

He came into Freddie's yard and said to me "I've had to pay another 7/6d for you but that's the last, 'cause the Magistrate said that from now onwards I can keep you away from school whenever I like."

Freddie had already paid me 7/6d for my day's work so I handed it over to father and said "There you are, that'll pay the fine." A broad smile came over his face as he took the money and I am quite sure that after he had paid the train fare and the fine, he had not got a penny left in his pocket.

After that, I never went to school again.

My schooldays in the early 1930's were a period of great poverty and hardship, in the Fens just as in the rest of the country. There was very little money to be earned, thousands of men were unemployed and many children were poorly fed, some must have been near to starvation. Somehow my parents always contrived to clothe us adequately and I know that I speak for my twelve brothers and sisters when I say that we never once went to bed feeling hungry, unless we were sent there without food as a punishment for some wrong-doing. Then all we were given was a drink of water.

8

By today's standards our diet was plain and lacked variety. Mother toiled over a black leaded cooking range to provide us with filling and nutritious food. She never failed to give us a three course meal once in the day.

Living in the country we had a large garden which provided a plentiful supply of potatoes and vegetables. From the cows we always had a good supply of milk. Once a week mother made butter from cream skimmed from the milk during the previous few days.

There was always a sack of flour in the house which mother used for making bread and puddings. One of her specialities was 'nothing' pudding which was the best way she knew of making a small quantity of meat stretch sufficiently to feed and satisfy the whole family. The pudding, which was from 14 to 16 inches long, was wrapped in a bag or cloth and boiled in a large pan. We ate slices of it with gravy if there was any, or with home made butter or even with brown sugar sprinkled over it.

A typical meal for Sunday lunch would start with Yorkshire pudding eaten either with butter, brown sugar or gravy. This was followed with another piece of Yorkshire pudding, with a small piece of meat, vegetables and gravy. After this we had a pudding made with milk and rice or tapioca or something similar.

Sometimes we had a special treat if father shot a duck and gave it to mother to cook instead of selling it.

Until I was 14, I had to be in bed by 6 o'clock with my brothers and sisters. Mother had a routine for getting us ready to go to bed. It was the youngest first and while one was being washed the next one had to be getting undressed ready. There was no tap in the house so all the water had to be carried in, in buckets. As there was no sink we had a small bath on the table. This was used for bathing the babies and small children, and used for washing in by the older ones. Water had to be heated in a kettle or saucepan on the open fire.

As soon as we were ready for bed we were sent upstairs with a candle, the only source of light on dark evenings. The moment we were in bed we had to blow it out and go to sleep. If we made any noise we were scolded by mother or father and soon got a spanking if we were not quiet.

When we were older we stayed up late and played cards or dominoes as we did not have a radio and of course there was no television. Mother spent most of her evenings working with a sewing machine making clothes for us. Sometimes she would be cutting down clothes which either she or father could no longer wear, in order to make something for one of us. Occasionally she bought a piece of material for making up into a dress or shirt. It was really to save money that she made all our clothes.

All the water for washing had to be fetched from the Hundred Foot river before she could start to heat the copper for her weekly wash. She had no spin drier so had to use her judgement on the weather for hanging things out to dry. When it was ready for ironing she used a box iron which

9

contained a triangular piece of iron which could be heated in the embers of a fire. When adjudged to be hot enough it was taken out of the fire with long tongs and popped into the box of the iron. It was easy to scorch clothes and aggravating when the iron cooled off and had to be re-heated. When there was only a small amount of ironing to do she used a flat iron which could be heated by putting it on the hob near to the fire.

Life was hard for mother when we were all young. She had no labour-saving devices and virtually everything had to be done by hand. She always considered her place was in the home and I can never remember returning from school and finding she was out. If married women did not work today children would not be as much trouble in schools, there would be less hooliganism and of course there would be far fewer people registered as unemployed.

2. Starting Work

For the first year after I left school I spent my days either working for father or doing casual work on nearby farms. During most of the summer I worked with him on the washes cutting thistles, ragwort and other weeds; digging out ditches; repairing gates and fences and looking after the horses, cattle and sheep which various farmers sent to graze on the pasture.

At harvest time I had no difficulty in getting a job leading horses on a large farm. The harvest was done on piece-work and the sooner it was finished the more the men earned, and the quicker they were paid. There was a bustle in the fields with men hurrying about their work so that no time was wasted.

One day when we were carting the shocks straight to the drum for threshing, I lost control of the horse I was leading and an absolute catastrophe was only narrowly avoided. It was customary while a cart was being unloaded for the bit to be taken from the horse's mouth and then hooked under its jaw, enabling it to feed easily. On this particular occasion, when perhaps I was being rather too slow for the men, one called out "Come on lad, git that horse out of the way quick!"

In my anxiety to do as I was told, forgetting to put the bit back, I began to tug on the lead. The horse, reluctant to leave the food it had been given, was loth to start, with the result that I tugged until the bridle came over its head. We used bridles with blinkers on them and as soon as these were removed the horse could see what was going on around it, took fright and bolted. I held on as long as I could but it was hopeless because when the horse could see as well as hear the cart rattling behind, it panicked even more.

Round the back of the tackle, across the field it went, as it made for home. It passed through the gateway at a full gallop and such was its momentum that it could not turn on the road but instead went straight across, coming to a stop upside down in the deep ditch on the other side.

The men were soon on the scene, trying to release the horse and calm it down. The blacksmith, whose shop was nearby, heard the commotion and came to see what was happening. He was soon at work with his hammer and chisel cutting the chains and chest thong as the collar, held tightly against the horse's throat, was threatening to choke it.

It took nine men to free the horse and pull it up on to the bank. They then lifted the cart out but unfortunately for me, it was easier to get horse and cart out on the far side of the ditch. This meant that I had to take it a long way round to get back to the farm. By this time the horse was as calm as a lamb. The horse and cart had been borrowed from Mr. Fletcher, who could see that the incident was not really my fault and therefore was not cross with me.

In the winter I milked the cows and did the milk round. When the Welney road was flooded, father borrowed a boat from Tommy Rudland to get the milk across. This gave me a chance to earn a few shillings by using the boat to ferry people from one side to the other.

As father could not afford to pay me for working for him I earned very little money during the year so I thought I would try and find some regular work. Most of the lads when they left school had no alternative to working on the land. Of course, I followed the general trend and decided to ask the foreman at Butchers Hill Farm for work. Teddy Bartrum had the reputation of being one of the best foremen in the Fens so naturally I was delighted when he said he would set me on. "How much will you pay me?" I asked with some timidity. "Eleven shillings a week. Start at seven, leave off at half past four during the week, four o'clock on Saturday. Half an hour for dockey between eleven and half past" came his sharp and firm reply, leaving me in no doubt that I could "take it or leave it."

Teddy Bartrum was strict and tough and did not hesitate to show his annoyance whenever I displeased him by giving me a sharp crisp clip across my ears, or if it was more convenient for him, he delivered a well-aimed boot to my backside.

When I started working at Butchers Hill, fenland farming was just beginning to recover from the depression which followed World War I. Profits were low and few farmers could afford to buy a tractor. Consequently most of the work was still done with horses and hand labour.

It was springtime and my first job was to lead the horse on a hoe in some sugar beet. A horse-hoe had four hoes, which removed weeds from between two rows of beet. Weeds and surplus plants within the row were later hoed out by hand. Sometimes the hoe man used a long handled hoe but in the Fens it was not uncommon for a short hoe to be used by a worker crawling on hands and knees up and down the rows. To make their work as easy as possible, the hoes on the horse-hoe were set close together so that only a narrow band of unmoved soil was left along the row. Steering the hoe called for skill and concentration and consequently, when the plants were small, a boy was employed to lead the horse leaving the hoe man free to look after the hoe. Later, when the crop was better grown, the horse could follow the rows and a leader was no longer necessary.

Another lad started work at the same time as I did and we were both sent horse hoeing. We soon discovered that there was an advantage in working with Charley as when dockey time came he rolled a cigarette for the lad leading his horse. Thus there was competition between us for Charley's favour. We soon realised that the first to arrive at the stables was chosen to go with him. We usually arrived at about 6 o'clock to help to groom the horses with curry combs and brushes while they were feeding. After that, we helped as best we could with harnessing the horses ready for the day's work. I tried hard to get there first each morning but was not always successful.

After the first week both of us were given a rise of one shilling a week, showing the foreman had been satisfied with our work.

When the sugar beet and mangolds had been singled, it was haymaking time which was followed after an interval of a few days by the corn harvest. As soon as the binder had done a few cuts round the field, men followed and stood the sheaves into shocks (or stooks) which were left long enough for the grain to ripen and harden before they were carted and stacked or threshed.

There was another time when a horse ran away from me. This was when we were carting muck from the yards. The dung and partly rotted straw was carted on to a corn field and made into a big well consolidated heap to ensure that it was well rotted before being spread on the stubble in the autumn. It was my job to lead the horse with a full cart to the heap and then take the empty cart back to the yard to meet another boy bringing the next full cart.

There was a man at the heap with a trace horse, which was used to help to pull the cart on to the top of the heap. Before going up, the tail board was taken out, enabling the load to be discharged by tipping the cart. After unloading, the trace horse was unhooked while I brought the tail board from the other side.

One day when I went round to get it, I made rather more noise than I should have done, causing the horse to take fright and run off. I ran forward to get hold of the lead but the horse had rather a hard mouth and was difficult to control. Teddy Bartrum, who was walking along the track, shouted "Hang on, don't let him go."

13

By now I was frightened and I shouted back "To hell with that, I'm not going to stand here and be run over" as I threw the line down.

There was no stopping the horse after this. It went across the track with the cart rattling and shaking behind and like the other horse, it made for its stable, smashing through a closed gate as it went. When it got to the stable door it went straight in without slowing down, finishing up with the shafts ripped from the cart dangling down beside it.

Teddy Bartrum came panting into the stable and soon left me in no doubt as to who was to blame on this occasion.

I continued to work on the land during the summer but in the autumn I was made yard boy.

The full-time yard man needed extra help at this time of the year as about 100 cattle were brought in from the washes where they grazed all summer, to be fattened in the yards. They were fed a mixture of waste potatoes cut up in a mangold slicer, soaked sugar beet pulp and chaff.

The food was piled on the floor, turned a time or two to mix it thoroughly, and then put into sacks which were handy for carrying into the yards and emptying into the wooden troughs. Feeding took about two hours and the remainder of the day was spent in carting straw for bedding and in getting the potatoes sliced ready for feeding in the evening and the following morning.

All the straw was stacked loose from the threshing drum and carting it on windy winter days required skill to avoid having too much of it blown away. As each forkful was pitched from the stack it had to be strategically placed on the cart by the loader, as he systematically built his load binding all the straw together. The journey to the yard was short but if the load was not well put together it could easily be thrown off as the cart lurched along the rutted tracks. How much easier straw carting is now when everything is in bales.

After working on the farm for a time I left to return to help father. I was reluctant to leave as I was happy, liked the work and got on well with the foreman but I realised the change would give me a chance to shoot wild-fowl and to catch plover, activities in which I had become very interested.

Father was shepherd of just over 400 acres of washes and when I was working for him he would sometimes have 200 horses in his care. Farmers sent all the horses they could spare to the washes as it was a cheap way of keeping them during the summer. They thrived on the permanent grass and after a rest of a few months were in good condition when required for the heavy work of root harvesting and autumn ploughing.

There are no fences in the washes, only ditches separate one field from another. It is not always possible to maintain a high enough water level to deter animals from trying to cross them and getting stuck in the soft mud. Twice daily father or I had to go round to see if the horses and cattle were safe. This had to be done mainly on foot although I used a bicycle on the drove and later, when I took over as shepherd after the war, I used a scramble motorcycle.

If I found a horse in the ditch I had to go all the way back to fetch father. He would get my uncle, William Richer Scott, who lived next door to come and help, and similarly we helped him when there was trouble on his washes.

It was difficult enough to cycle down the deeply rutted drove at any time but when we had halters, ropes and shovels to carry it became almost impossible. Getting a horse out of a ditch was no easy task but over the years father had gained so much experience that usually the three of us could pull it out.

An unbroken horse would be frightened by our approach and would immediately start to struggle, trying to get away. In this case, a halter was put on as quickly as possible and either I would hold it or it would be tied to a spade which had been knocked well into the soft peat.

As soon as the horse was securely tethered, father started to dig a hole in the side of the ditch near the animal's front legs. When this was finished, one pulling on the halter and two pushing behind might be sufficient to get it out.

Some horses, when they got into a ditch, struggled to get out and became exhausted before we could reach them. In cases like this, a cart rope was put round the horse's hind quarters under its tail and with a man on each end, it could usually be heaved out. On odd occasions, when all else failed, I was sent back to the village for more help.

Sheep had to be rounded up twice during the summer as it was compulsory to dip them twice in those days. The dips were not so persistent or effective as they are now and in spite of the dipping some of the sheep were struck by fly. If such an animal was spotted during our daily inspections it had to be caught, the maggots removed and a dressing applied.

The cattle were generally little trouble except when gadflies sent the terrified animals charging round the field, with tails raised in a frantic attempt to escape from the buzzing insects. There is virtually no shelter on the washes, as few trees survive the periodic flooding, so the cattle would try to get away by crossing a ditch.

This made extra work for us, as any animal stuck in the mud had to be pulled out and if our cattle had got mixed with our neighbours' cattle there was the difficult task of separating them again.

On days when the animals did not require attention, after I had done the milk round I helped father to mow thistles or clean out ditches. A freshly dug ditch, free from weed growth, was a good deterrent to the animals so we worked on the ditches whenever we had any spare time. It was very hard work in the still humid atmosphere of the washes but I enjoyed it for at the end of the day there was the great satisfaction of looking back on the day's achievements. Over and above this, I learned to love the loneliness of the washes. Apart from the call of the birds nothing disturbed the silence and there was the mixed smell of freshly dug mud, meadowsweet and other fragrant plants.

In the autumn, when there was less work to do on the washes, father let me help neighbours with the potato harvest. For a time I worked for my cousin, Ernie Kent, who had a holding on Colony Farm, Manea. The system was to spin the potatoes out with a horse drawn spinner. Women followed behind and picked the potatoes into baskets which were made in the village and called 'cobs'. A horse and cart, with a man walking alongside, went down the rows when the crop had been lifted and each full cob was thrown up to someone in the cart who emptied it and threw it down again, ready for refilling when the next row was lifted. I was usually the cob catcher as I was only a lad at the time and it was a fairly easy job.

Small Fen farmers often help each other and for many years Ernie worked with Russ Marshall during potato harvesting. One day it was decided that an extra horse would have to be brought back from the washes ready for the next day's work.

It was already getting dusk when Ernie rowed Russ across the river Delph. He then had to walk down to near Welney, where the horse was grazing near old Will Kent's cottage. In the gathering dusk he caught it and brought it back by road, a distance of several miles, so it was dark before the horse was in the stable and fed.

Early in the morning, before Ernie arrived, Russ yolked the horse and put it on the spinner alongside the two which had been at work the previous day. As soon as they started to work the noise frightened the new horse which bolted, and in doing so, frightened the other horses. Before they could be stopped the gears of the spinner were smashed beyond repair. It was only after the horses had calmed down that Ernie came along and realised Russ had caught the wrong horse.

When I was in my late teens, after work some evenings I helped Bert Page, who lived in Welney but worked for an Upwell butcher. On most Tuesday and Thursday evenings I cycled over to Upwell and helped him with killing animals in the small slaughter-house at the rear of the shop. A typical evening's killing was six pigs, two sheep and one bullock, which satisfied the needs of the shop for the next few days.

At the end of the evening he tied my bicycle on the back of his roundsman's van and brought me back. On fine summer evenings we stopped at Three Holes and swam naked in the river there. After we had dried ourselves, he took me to his home where his wife made us a hot drink before I eventually cycled back to Suspension Bridge about midnight.

On Saturdays Bert did his round in our hamlet, starting there about 9 o'clock in the evening. He had a bullnose Morris van in which he taught me to drive. His rounds included droves which were almost deserted so I could drive without any fear of being seen by the local policemen. Although I had no licence he let me drive and deliver to some of the isolated cottages while he stayed in one of the local pubs.

For a time Bert kept some greyhounds which he raced on the track at Newmarket Road, Cambridge. He had an Essex super-six car in which he

16

took George Smart (who worked for him), two greyhounds and me to the meetings. I helped to parade the dogs and took them up to the traps, while Bert put his bets on whichever dog took his fancy.

One evening, when he had one of his best dogs in a race, he was so sure that it would win that he put all the money he had with him on it. The price was 8 to 1 so he was hoping for a good win but it was not to be, as it only managed to come fourth.

After he had caught the dog and got back to the car he said "There's something wrong with that dog, I'll feed him up." I did not know what he meant by this until next time I was at the Butcher's shop at Welney and saw him give the dog an enormous feed. I knew very well it was far too much and asked "Whatever are you doing, giving him all that?" "You'll see!" he replied.

The next time we went racing the dog came last as he was far too fat and out of condition. After this, Bert gradually began to reduce the amount of food he gave it. The next time it raced the odds were 25 to 1 as nobody thought it was any good but it managed to finish third.

Bert decided it was now time to get the dog really fit. He got an old car, put it on to a grass field, jacked up the rear wheels and after taking the tyre and tube off one wheel, wound some wire rope round it. I then helped him to make a track round the field on which we could train his dog to the peak of fitness.

While Bert held the dog, I waited in the car for a signal to let the clutch in and wind up the rope, aiming to keep the 'hare' just ahead. Our training sessions were not an unqualified success as I sometimes let the 'hare' (which was a dead rabbit) go too slowly so the dog caught it. However, we did our best and when the next racing night came we were full of high hopes for success.

Bert gave me £1 to put on—10 shillings each way at 25 to 1 but as I was not so confident as Bert, I only had a shilling each way on Bert's dog and the same amount on a dog which I picked by shutting my eyes and running my finger down the list.

Our excitement mounted as the hare started round the track, the trap doors flew open and Bert's dog soon took the lead. Unfortunately, the hare broke down and when the race was re-run, our dog would not go at all and finished last. That night on the way home I paid for the drinks from the money won on my other bet.

Disappointed, but undaunted, Bert decided to buy a greyhound which was advertised in a newspaper. It had to come from the north somewhere so arrangements were made to have it sent by train to Peterborough North Station. On the Saturday it was due to arrive, I helped Bert to finish his round early to enable us to get to the station by 9 o'clock.

We were delayed a little and as there was nobody to look after the dog, a porter sent it on to Peterborough South Station. We raced across the city but again, were too late as we discovered it had been left on the train and consigned to Manea station. Bert, unable to conceal his annoyance, swore at the unfortunate porter who had only tried to be helpful, before we scrambled into the car to chase the train to Manea.

The train arrived there first and for some reason which I never understood, the station master decided that the train should stop at the level crossing near Manea village to leave the dog in the care of the keeper. At last we caught up with it, after having travelled about 60 miles, when we could just have waited for it at Manea. It was nearly 2 o'clock in the morning when we got there as I distinctly remember the crossing keeper putting his clock forward at the hour, it being the night when summer time commenced.

All our efforts were of little avail as the dog never lived up to the description in the advertisement and Bert never won a race with it.

Bert was always very kind to me. Whenever he had a chance to take me for a ride in his car on his half-day holiday, he did so. In this way I visited various seaside towns and other places in the area which I would not have had a chance to see had it not been for Bert. In those days few people had a car and it was a rare treat to be taken out in one.

3. Old Will

From the time that I lived with my great uncle, Will Kent, while my knee
was healing, I was a regular visitor to his lonely cottage. I always called
him "Old Will" to distinguish him from my uncle, Will Kent. He was a
typical "Fen Tiger", fiercely independent, with a temper that was easily
roused but slow to calm down again. Sometimes I would be sitting by the
fireside talking to my great aunt and their daughter Polly when he came
home still very angry about something that had happened during the day.
More often than not he would be so late that I would already have gone
home before he returned.

Their little timber cottage was in the washes, quite close to the Hundred
Foot river, not far from Toll Corner. Although it was possible to walk up
the bank drove, the usual way of getting there was to cross the river in a
punt. Everybody knew that if they wanted to visit or to deliver anything,
all that was necessary was to stand on the top of the bank and call my
great aunt.

She would come hurrying out, her long skirts dragging on the ground as
she walked through the muddy silt to get into the punt. This was 16-20
feet long made from solid planks, well tarred to keep out the water. I
remember that when a new one was needed my uncle, Will Kent, com-
pleted the whole job in three days.

To cross the river the punt was pushed with a good stout willow pole into the tide. It would then be carried across to the other bank with only a few paddling strokes on the pole. If the punt was started off to go with the tide it might finish 200 or 300 yards away.

Each day Auntie took her daughter across as she worked on a farm nearly opposite to where they lived. Farmers wanting to cross to look at their cattle, first gave a shout and then she fetched them, and of course she was at old Will's beck and call.

Since the cottage was actually in the washes it was frequently flooded during the winter. As the water rose, all the furniture was carried upstairs or piled on to a table. Then with a few belongings, the family left to stay with Jarmin Smart at Welney, or at the Carpenter's Arms, Suspension Bridge.

When old Will was not at work he could be found in a pub. I saw him mostly in the Carpenter's Arms as I did not often go into any of the other pubs in those days. There were a number of games which I used to enjoy watching him play because he had acquired skill at them due, no doubt, to the practice which he had playing them regularly.

I remember once seeing old Will score 19 out of 20 on the bull ringle. This was very popular at the time. The player had to throw a ring hung on string from the ceiling, on to a hook fixed on the wall. He used to play another game which consisted of throwing small bags of beans through holes in a big sloping board. There was also "penny in the hole". The "hole" was in one of the wooden seats and the player stood a short distance away, trying to throw as many pennies through the hole as possible. Shove ha'penny was also played but like all the other games was mostly played only by the older men.

In the cold days of winter these men drank "poker" beer. A large poker, kept for the purpose, was put into the fire until it was red hot then, after a quick wipe on an old brush, was plunged into the pint of beer. Sometimes a small knob of ginger root was added as this was regarded as a good preventative or cure for a cold. Of course, there was also a spitoon full of sawdust for the benefit of the tobacco chewers.

One lunch time I happened to be in the Carpenter's Arms when old Will came in. He was in a terrible rage because he could not find his gun rod which he used for ramming wadding into his punt gun. As he entered he cried out furiously "Someone's pinched my bloody gun rod" thinking that someone had taken it just to annoy him.

After a good amount of shouting and arguing he was finally convinced that nobody had taken it. The landlord, Sammy Roult, offered to go down to the bank with him to search for it. They had a careful look round the spot where the gun was normally fixed on the bank but found no trace. Eventually, Sammy found some small fragments of the rod some distance away.

What had probably happened was that old Will had been drunk, or nearly so, when he had last loaded the gun and had forgotten to take the

20

rod out after ramming the wadding in. No doubt when he next went to the gun he fired it without realising the rod was still in the barrel, although he never admitted doing so.

One day, when there was about 2 to 2ft. 6 inches of water on the Welney road, old Will decided that he wanted some new wellingtons. Alfred James, who operated a ferry boat for the postman and anybody else who wanted to cross, took him over the river but during the journey an argument developed. When they arrived on the Welney side, Alfred said, "You awkward old so-and-so, now I won't take you back, you'll have to walk."

Undaunted, old Will said "I can do that easily enough" and that is just what he did after he had finished his shopping. When he got back to Suspension Bridge he walked straight into the Crown. As he squelched up to the bar someone shouted "You look a bit wet Will." To this he replied "Yes, I am, a little" as he took off his wellingtons and emptied the water on to the floor. He then turned out his pockets which were also full of water. Poor Saul Malkin dared not complain for fear of the consequences of any further provocation. Old Will spent the rest of the evening drying out in front of the fire, unperturbed by the steam rising all round him.

Wildfowlers like old Will never seemed to have any fear of gunpowder, probably because they did not realise how dangerous it could be. In the early days of punt gunning, when flintlock guns were used, for a successful firing the gunpowder had to be absolutely dry. Many a time I have been in his cottage and seen a good double handful of hay being dried on the black cooking range, for use as wadding, with a 5 lb. tin of gunpowder standing nearby. Sometimes there would be a 1 lb. cardboard packet of priming powder standing on the stove.

In a cupboard just to the right of the cooking range he kept his powder and at times there must have been as much as 20 lbs. there. Whenever he went to the cupboard he would say "Must keep it dry bor, no good if you get out there and your powder isn't dry."

The fire was usually of coal but wood was also burnt and it would only have needed a spark on the priming powder to have blown the whole house up.

Old Will never had an accident in this way but Tommy Rudland did. For most of his married life he lived with his wife in a little cottage near the bank of the Old Bedford river but when she died he went to live in the village. He retained possession of the cottage and used it for a workshop for making eel hives, knitting plover nets and various other jobs.

After one or two unsuccessful punt gunning trips he realised the trouble was that he was using damp gunpowder. He took it to his cottage and after making a roaring fire spread it out on a newspaper on the table. A spark must have ignited it because there was a dreadful explosion which blew the room to pieces. Tommy was found crawling out of the door with black gunpowder marks all over his face.

He was in hospital for a very long time. In those days public benefits were very small so whist drives were held in the village to raise funds to support him while he was unable to make a living for himself.

21

There was a long low oak beam in old Will's living room on which he kept his 12-bore guns. There was one gun on each side. One large nail supported the butt end and a small one supported the barrel. Although there was only about $\frac{1}{4}$ inch clearance between the trigger guard and the nail head, the guns were usually put up loaded.

On days when I knew that old Will was away I would persuade my great aunt to let me get one of the guns down on the pretext of wanting to kill a carrion crow which was worrying the mallard which were kept in a pen at the rear of the cottage. My real intention, in fact, was to go looking for a pheasant or wild duck. As I carefully manoeuvered a gun down from the beam, scared stiff in case I accidentally set it off, she would say "Do be careful, it's probably loaded."

The first time that I went after wildfowl I wandered around but could not get a shot until I realised that the ducks were all coming in to old Will's plover splash. I went over to his plover netting hide and I had not long settled there when some mallard came in and I was able to shoot my first duck. The sun was going down but before the light failed completely I had four ducks from five shots and I was very pleased with myself.

When I returned to the cottage my aunt was surprised to see the ducks and exclaimed "Where did you get them from?" "Well I stood round Uncle Will's splash and just shot them as they came in" I replied. "Oh" she said "You'll get into a hell of a row when he comes in 'cos he don't like anyone shooting round his splash, he reckons it puts the plover off."

I waited for him to come home, not daring to think what he would say but in the end he was not as cross as I expected. Nevertheless, I knew better than to do it again. The real reason for his concern was that shooting disturbed the plover, some of which moved around at night. If they were put off then the number which came in during the next day or two was very much reduced.

After the end of one shooting season old Will was walking along the Cradge bank when he managed, quite unexpectedly, to get a shot at some wigeon. He brought two of them down and was busy picking them up when he saw Bert Dowsby who worked for the Great Ouse River Board, coming towards him. When they met, Bert said "Will, these ducks are not good at this time of the year" Will replied "And why not?". "Well, the season's finished" "That may be so but there's more gravy in them than there is in 'taters." said old Will as he went back to his cottage, pleased that he would be having duck rather than rabbit or hare for his dinner.

4. Plover Netting

As autumn approached, in the year that I went back to work for father, I began to take an even keener interest in the movement of ducks about the washes and in the ditches, as I knew that the shooting season commenced on 12th August (it is different now) and I wanted to know where I had the best chance of getting them when the time came.

I had my first gun licence when I was 14 so by the time I rejoined father I had already been shooting for two seasons. As soon as the season started, whenever I had a spare moment, I was out with my gun, walking round the washes in the early morning as the sun rose over the Hundred Foot river, or late in the evening as it sank behind Welney village. I could usually get a pair or two of mallard but in the early part of the season they had to be plucked, cleaned and eaten quickly. If I was lucky I sold a pair or two locally but it was too mild to send them to London although the price was good. It would be much easier to dispose of them now that most house-holders have refrigerators and many with deep-freeze cabinets would buy for later use.

In late summer the plovers, which nested on the washes and neighbour-ing farmland, joined together into large flocks. Their comings and goings I also noted for at the beginning of September the plover netting season began.

Plover catching, a tradition in the washes, only ceased when it was made illegal in 1947. Originally, when the Fens were poorly drained, there was enough flooded pasture for the catcher to set his nets. As drainage improved, flooding became less frequent and of shorter duration, forcing the professionals to use areas of specially prepared grassland for their plover netting.

Some of the washes were ideal as there were slackers, or small sluices, which could be used if necessary to flood an area and maintain the water depth at 6 to 8 inches.

Father always established his splash of water on a particular field, which is now owned by the Wildfowl Trust, and because of its former use is still called 'Plover Wash.' The first thing he did was to make an island 22 yards long and 4 feet wide in a part of the washes where the water was the right depth. The outside was formed from sods of turf while the middle part was filled with grass which had been freshly mown. The 8-foot wide net was the same length as the island and was made of super-fine dark thread with 3 inch mesh. At each end there was a pole which was attached to a piece of cart spring. The metal springs were forced into the ground and when the net was set, they were held under tension by rope and pegs driven in near the corner of the net. The tension could be released by a line about 200 yards long, which ran through pulleys to a small hide of reed hurdles, made on the edge of a ditch. When released, the net swung through 180 degrees, hopefully entangling any plovers that were on the island.

When the washes were flooded, a floating bed was used by some of the netters. It was made up from four sections each 5 yards long and 4 feet wide. The sections, made with a wooden framework covered with wire netting, were buoyant enough to float. They could be joined together and towed behind a punt and then secured in a suitable position.

After covering the wire netting with freshly cut grass and setting the net, the netter concealed himself behind a portable hide made of reed hurdles or willow sticks. Each night the floating bed had to be taken to a high piece of ground where it could be made safe, as there was no way of knowing how much the water level would change before it would be used again.

To attract plovers, two devices were used. Firstly, two kinds of decoys were used. Stuffed skins of dead plovers were put about the island as if they were feeding. Live decoys were tethered nearby on sods of turf or stools on which they could perch. They could be made to flutter by pulling on the watch line which was joined to a piece of string and elastic to which the birds were tied. A pull on the line caused the decoy momentarily to lose balance and as it fluttered to regain its perch, it exposed some of the white and more conspicuous parts of its wing. This helped to encourage flocks of plovers flying over to settle within the catching areas.

At the beginning of each season, some of the first caught plovers were kept for use as live decoys. Some netters left their decoys out all the time but they were sometimes killed by rats. Father kept his in a chicken run, feeding them on worms or finely cut strips of shin beef.

24

The second means used to entice the plovers down was a whistle, made from a little hollow piece of elder with a small fragment of willow set into it to act as a reed. The netter watched the flocks of plover as they left their feeding grounds in the Fens and when they came overhead, from within his hide, he worked his decoys and called on his whistle.

From a very early age I can remember going with my father and sitting with him in his hide while he was plover catching. Riding on the cross-bar of his bicycle was a hazardous but adventurous journey along the bank drove. Gradually, he taught me all the wiles of the craft but my greatest thrill was when he told me one September morning that I could go plover catching after I had finished milking.

Either through my lack of experience, or because it was not a very good season, catches were low. October came and I was still only getting 9 or 10 birds for each pull.

On Sunday, when I went to have lunch with my Great Aunt, she asked me "How have you been getting on this week?" "Not very well" I replied, rather despondently. She was a keen observer of the fenland skies and knew from past experience the conditions which favoured plover catching' "Well, you'll get some good pulls from now on" she said.

Sure enough, on the next day when I awoke to a red sky after overnight rain, there were some big flocks of plovers on the move.

A particularly large flock, which had been feeding on a potato field, got up and wheeled overhead just as I got back into the hide. I worked my decoys and blew on the whistle and eventually a group of about 50, which left the main flock, settled on the island. When I pulled the line, the net sprang over, trapping 38 birds to give me my first experience of a good pull. My luck continued for the rest of the day and I ended with a bag of 120, which pleased me immensely.

One afternoon, when I was not catching many birds, I could see that Tommy Rudland, who was about half a mile from me, was doing very much better. The net I was using had a large number of holes but as it was too old to be worth mending father had bought a new one. Being youthful and inexperienced I thought I could change the nets over in a matter of a few minutes.

The new net, which had diamond mesh, already had a line threaded through it. Foolishly I pulled it out thinking I could easily thread it on to the old line. I got the nets into a terrible tangle and try as I would, I could not untangle them. Plovers were flying all round me but I could not set my net.

In desperation I got on my bicycle and went to Tommy for help. When I showed him the nets he said "Cor blast bor, however did you git this in such a muddle?" While he untangled them he let me have a go with his net but I did not catch anything. He told me exactly how to fix the new net but after I had caught about 15 birds the flight was over so I ended up by having a very poor day.

25

When I explained to father what had happened I neither expected, nor got, any sympathy. He merely said "Why ever didn't you let Tommy fix it in the first place?" I thought that it is always easy to be wise after the event, but dare not say so.

After each pull, the birds were first killed then disentangled from the net and laid out to dry on a bank near the hide. As dusk approached, plovers ceased flying in any numbers and it was time to go home. The net had to be carefully taken up and hung out to dry. Both live and dead decoys were gathered up to be kept for use next day. The day's catch was put into a sack and carried home.

If the catch had been good, it was despatched immediately but if there were not enough to send off they were laid out on the quarry tiled floor of our pantry. All the plovers were sold in London as were most of the ducks.

When we had 100 to 120 plovers father packed them into a one-hundred-weight seed potato sack which we used for despatching. Provided each bird had its head neatly tucked under it's wing and care was taken to arrange them in the sack, 120 could be packed in. Sometimes there might only be 60 to 70 plovers and then 9 to 10 ducks were put in to fill the sack.

Everything was sent by train, either from Hilgay or Littleport station. Hilgay was slightly closer, being about five miles away but sometimes it was more convenient to go to Littleport. With the sack balanced rather precariously on the handlebars, father or I would cycle off to catch the train which left a few minutes after 6 o'clock in the evening. The plovers were then in London early the next day and a cheque in payment would arrive the following day.

Before the Second World War, plovers were sold at 2½d to 3d each. At a time when agricultural workers' wages were 28/- to 30/- per week, a catch of 100 plovers in two or three days represented good payment.

While I was working with father I had two seasons plover catching. I went whenever the weather was suitable. The only times I was unable to go was when the whole wash was flooded and the water was too deep and when it was frosty. It was then impossible to continue as the net so easily became frozen to the grass and into the water. The best pulls were when it was wet and stormy. The plover which had been feeding on sticky ploughed land seemed to like to return, every now and again, to clean themselves in the splash of water.

Father took all the money for the plovers. He could not afford to pay me as the family was growing very large and there were many mouths to feed.

I had some more seasons plover catching on my own or with one of my uncles. In 1939, just after war broke out, I was catching with my uncle, George Kent, on his stretch of land. We sent a few small packages away and to our surprise we only got 1d each for them. We tried again but still only got 1d and decided it was not worthwhile at that price. This was the lowest price I ever remember plovers fetching.

5. Punt Gunning

I always hoped that Old Will would teach me how to punt gun but he never did. The first man to let me fire his gun was Tommy Rudland, a well-known professional wildfowler who lived in Welney. He had an old punt and gun and one day he said to me "Come on bor, have a go."

I was thrilled and delighted but scared stiff. Often I had watched as he set out in his slender craft with a massive punt gun balanced on it. There seemed so little of the punt above water but later I realised that this was essential because the gunner, when lying flat, had to be able to paddle with his hands on both sides of the punt.

After what seemed to be an interminable time as I sat on the bank watching his slow progress across the water, there was a huge puff of smoke followed by a tremendous flapping of wings of ducks which had escaped the shoot or had been disturbed. Moments later the report of the gun echoed across the water.

I suppose the element of fear gave added zest as I set off for the first time, although it was really only a dummy run so that I could get the feel of both punt and gun. For my first two outings Tommy loaded with the usual amount of powder but used no shot to make sure there was no kick or rebound when I fired.

After the two trials Tommy said "I think you are ready to have a proper go now." Even then he only loaded with a half pound of shot instead of the usual threequarters. From the barrier bank of the Old Bedford river we had a good clear view across the washes, which were flooded to within a 100 yards of the Hundred Foot river. We could see several rafts of ducks floating about, bobbing up and down on the small ruffled waves which disturbed the surface of the water.

As I settled down into the punt, Tommy explained what I should do to approach a group of about 12 mallard, some 400 yards from where we were. He tried to tell me how to stalk, them but I felt so confident that I should get within range without any difficulty that his words fell on deaf ears. With all the assurance and optimism of youth, I set off, paddling across the water straight towards the duck.

I went quite steadily, hardly seeming to make a ripple with the paddles, until the ducks seemed as large as geese as I looked down the length of the barrel to keep it lined up with the centre of the group. When I judged I was well within range, with fear and trepidation, I pulled the trigger expecting, when the smoke cleared, to see the mutilated remains of ducks floating ahead of me. In fact, when the smoke cleared, there was not a duck in sight, nor was there a single feather to be seen.

When I got back to the bank Tommy, who possessed the countryman's characteristic of patience combined with firmness when instructing the young, told me that I would never kill ducks like that. He explained that my approach, especially in the last 100 yards, would have to be much slower if I was to get within the range of ducks or geese.

"I was right on top of them and straight for them" I protested, but Tommy was adamant that I was not within 150 yards of them and therefore well out of range.

The same thing happened on the next four occasions but then one afternoon my luck changed. It was clear, with a hazy winter sun low over the washes. There was hardly a ripple on the water on which some large groups of wigeon were sitting out.

I was anxious to succeed but my determination was heightened when Tommy said "Now this time you must get something or I shan't let you use my punt again." He sent me off, paddling into the sun, telling me to aim towards a spot where a bank was showing above the water. He intended me to go beyond the ducks until I could turn and stalk towards them with my back to the sun.

"When you start towards them you will hear me talking, listen carefully and I'll tell you just what to do" he said. I thought this sounded rather stupid as I felt sure that if he spoke loud enough for me to hear, he would disturb the ducks. However, I should have known better than to doubt him.

As I started to paddle away I was afraid I would not hear what he was saying but when he started to talk I was surprised how clearly his voice carried, and I was easily able to follow his instructions. He told me to go north, which meant that I was going towards the ducks with the sun behind me. I paddled along steadily for about three minutes, after which I heard him say "Watch the wigeon carefully now and every time any heads are lifted stop paddling until they settle again.

It looked to me as if I was about 100 yards from the ducks when he said "Stop". After a while he said "Go on again", followed a moment later by "Stop". From the shore he was keeping a sharp watch and whenever the ducks showed signs of restlessness he would tell me to stop and not allow me to carry on again until they had all settled. During the 20 minutes which I spent following his commands I realised how impatient I had been on my earlier outings.

I thought I would soon be running into the ducks but dared not fire until he gave the order. At last he said "Go steady now, aim for the thickest part of the ducks and be ready to fire when I tell you."

The punt glided slowly onward, there was a slight ripple of waves against the bows, otherwise there was not a sound. As soon as I heard him say "Fire" I obeyed the command, breaking the silence with the monstrous report from the gun, which kicked back knocking me back at the same time before it rolled over. Luckily it neither capsized the punt nor went overboard.

When the smoke had cleared I could see four or five wigeon lying dead about 60 to 70 yards ahead. I paddled forward, picked up the dead ducks and then rounded up the cripples and killed them as I knew that the unbreakable rule of the punt gunners on the washes was never to leave any wounded birds behind. It was a wonderful feeling to paddle back to show Tommy the results of our combined efforts.

Now that I had shown that I could successfully use a punt gun, old Will gave me a gun called 'Bacca Jack", which had belonged to a Christchurch blacksmith and must have been well over 100 years old when it was given to me. Gutty See, one of the famous Welney professional skaters loaned me a small punt and thus I was equipped to make a start as a professional punt gunner.

In the autumn and early winter of the year that I was given 'Bacca Jack' there was no flood water but I could not wait to use it so decided I would set it up as a bank gun. This meant putting it on the highest part of a bank overlooking a splash of water. I made a few little reed hurdles about two feet high which, when held in position with a few tussocks of grass, were sufficient to hide the gun.

In order to reach the gun I used the punt along one of the ditches, then crawled on my stomach until I was screened from the ducks by the bank. The gun was always on the north side of the splash to make sure that I could shoot looking towards the moon. When the ducks approached at night they could then be seen silhouetted while I was not easily seen by them.

As decoys I used a few live mallard tethered in the area. They were not harmed by the shot as the gun was aimed at ducks as they rose from the water. Sometimes I had some success but on many a cold night I have waited for hours, crouched behind the reed screen while the ducks flew all round me but none stopped near enough for me to have a shot at them.

Most of the shepherds did some punt gunning when there was sufficient water. They would go out in the morning and again in the evening. Between times they might earn a shilling or two by ferrying people from one side of the washes to the other when the road was impassable, or spend a few coppers at the Lamb and Flag or the Three Tuns.

Each shepherd only shot over the washes for which he was responsible. This was a sensible arrangement as it avoided the risk of two punt gunners approaching the same ducks with the consequent danger of firing towards each other.

I was able to use my father's washes, unless he had given someone else permission to do so. As soon as there was enough flood water when the shooting season had started, whenever possible I went out in my punt. In the morning, if I was not sure where to find some ducks, I walked along the bank until I knew where the biggest groups were. Then I went to get the punt and gun ready for the day's expedition.

Overnight it was customary to leave the gun on two pieces of wood, covering the lock with a sack or an odd piece cut from a wellington boot. To cover the gun, the punt was turned upside down over it.

In the morning the punt was turned over and pushed about halfway into the water. The gun was then put with the barrel on a small block at the bow, the stock resting on the 'shoe'. This was a wedge-shaped piece of wood large enough for the gunner to rest his chest on when lying down to paddle the punt. To make it softer I sometimes added some padding in the shape of a hay-filled bag placed underneath some old sacks.

Although the stock was resting on the shoe, it was not fixed and had to be kept steady by pushing one's chest up against it. It was therefore essential only to fire the gun when there was sufficient water for the punt to take the recoil. If the gun was fired while the back of the punt was near to a bank, the recoil was taken on the chest. I have been severely bruised in this way on a number of occasions.

I can remember several times, when I was punting down a narrow dyke, turning ever so slightly to get a better shot, not realising that there was land immediately behind me when I fired. The stock brushed against my shirt buttons as it kicked back, making a very sore strip down my chest. A similar thing happened if I forgot to turn my head away from the gun quickly enough to avoid the flash in the pan, and again I was heavily bruised by the kick as the gun recoiled.

Unlike coastal punt gunners, the gunners on the washes did not rope their guns. The rather larger and stronger punts used on the coast and estuaries were necessary because of the rougher water encountered. To hold the gun, it was securely roped at the bow and round the stock, thus ensuring that all the recoil was taken by the punt. On the washes we made shorter trips and really found it was too much bother to rope the gun as it would then have had to be untied three or four times a day for reloading. Also, our punts were not strong enough to have the gun roped to them.

Ernie James was, as far as I know, the only man who used a rope on the washes. After a number of fairly severe knocks on his chest, followed by a period of illness, he had a special punt made for the purpose. I fired it on occasions and I must admit that I found it easier as I could get lower in the punt and have my head much closer to the stock since there was no fear of harmful effects from the recoil.

The gun was usually left loaded overnight so that in the morning all that had to be done was to put it on the punt and set off in search of the duck. The depth of water was often the determining factor in deciding which ducks to go for. I got to know just where I could go by looking at the height of the water on the marker near Welney bridge. If it was only 104 then some fields could not be shot over but by the time it reached 105, most of the washes were accessible.

Having decided which ducks to go for I worked out how I could get as close as possible down the ditches under cover of the banks. To get into a field I used the deeper water where a groove had been cut to take water from the lowest part of the washes into the ditches. It was only necessary to turn into the groove and go a short distance into the field in order to get a good shot

When going down the river and main ditches I used flat paddles, about four inches wide, the size of a cricket bat with handles about six to nine inches long. Lying down, it was possible to use one on each side of the punt. The paddles were never taken out of the water. After each stroke, a turn of the wrist brought the narrow edge in line ready for the forward movement.

In shallow water I pushed my punt forward with stalking sticks about five feet long. These had short tines from a cut off pitch fork, to give a grip on the flooded grassland. Near the bottom of the wooden shaft there was a heavy lead weight or sinker which served two purposes. Firstly, it made it easier for the punter to keep his sticks down in the water by counteracting the tendency for them to float. Secondly, when the punt was near enough to the ducks, the sticks could be released without taking them from the water, as in the upright position in which they were held by the sinker, they drifted very little and could easily be recovered after the gun had been fired.

It is often said that punt gunners were murderers but this is absolutely untrue. As soon as the gun had been fired, the practice was to rise to one's knees and keep a watch on all the ducks which had not been killed. The position of wounded ducks that were still able to fly before dropping had to be noted so that they could be walked up later and, if necessary, shot with a 12-bore.

One kept an eye on cripples, looking to right and left and marking the spot where they disappeared from sight. Crippled ducks will always make for cover, never for deep water. As I was normally shooting on water surrounded by ditches, it was easy to see where they made for and find them later. Providing you were careful it was possible to pick up nearly every bird which had been killed or wounded.

31

Sometimes when a duck had gone into a ditch and I had not been able to find it, I told two older men, Cutty See and Joey Butcher, that if they went and walked along a certain ditch they would find a cripple which should be easy to shoot for their dinner.

For me, punt gunning was a genuine method of wildfowling and for many of us before the war it was the only way we had of making a living during the winter. There was no indiscriminate shooting. The object was to kill as many as possible with each shot as the more you had to sell, the better your income.

Re-loading was only possible on land. The gun was taken from the firing position, lifted forward, and turned over so that the barrel was protruding well out of the punt and pointing slightly upwards.

After each shot or two, the first thing to do was to wash the barrel out. This was done by winding a piece of rag on to the worm of the ramrod which was kept in the punt. After dipping it into the water it was pushed up and down the barrel to remove all the residues of black powder. The only time when the barrel was not washed out was at the end of the season as the coating of powder helped to protect it from corroding and rusting during the spring and summer. Before the first shot of the season, a thorough washing with boiling water and caustic soda was needed to remove the accumulated powder and dust.

On most of the guns the lock could be removed easily by undoing two bolts and thus it was not affected during the process of washing out. The touch hole in the barrel was cleaned with a cut off feather kept in your cap or budget. The budget was a holder made from leather tucked into a wooden base of 14 to 18 inches diameter in which powder, shot, caps, priming powder, rag and other necessities were kept.

After the barrel had been thoroughly dried, a feather stalk was put into the touch hole and loading could begin. Firstly the powder was measured out into a charger. This was made from a cow horn and held about two ounces. The powder was tipped in and the barrel gently tapped to make sure that it was all at the bottom. Next a wad, made from soft fine meadow hay, was rammed in with a rod. The tighter this was rammed in, the better the killing power of the shot but the greater the kick.

Following this, the same charger was used for measuring the shot. It was not quite filled as the aim was to have about "a clay pipe full" less by volume of shot than powder.

The shot, which weighed about one pound, was held in position by another wad. This was smaller than the powder wad and the minimum necessary to stop the shot from moving was used. It was rammed lightly as if it was too tight, "balling" of the shot occurred when it was fired.

The gun could be left in this state but before it could be fired it had to be primed. This was done by taking the feather from the touch hole and gently pushing priming powder from the pan through the hole with a hair or hat pin. The fine priming powder was then in contact with the much coarser gunpowder and the gun was ready for firing.

Ducks, mallard, wigeon and pintail were the usual target, chiefly because geese were not worth shooting. On the London market they only made 6d.

Suspension Bridge, Welney *(from an old postcard)*

My sister Sylvia
doing the milk round

My daughter Carolyn and my brother Aubrey (right)
helping with some foot rot treatment.

Sometimes the ewes need extra food if grazing is short

This photograph was taken during the war, so that a copy could be sent to me, while I was a P.O.W.

When the family were on the bus going to Ely to have it taken, Mother was asked for identity cards, and was able to produce all 14 from her handbag.

THE SCOTT FAMILY

Punt Gunning *(photo Terry Andrew Artha)*

Welney Wildfowl refuge — the first task was to dig a lagoon *(photo Ted Eales)*

Feeding the swans (*photo* *Beryl Jolly*)

In the Lamb & Flag, after an evening flight

The new bridge of the Hundred Foot river giving access to the observatory
(photo H. J. Mason)

Bewick's Swans feeding on winter wheat in front of Butcher's Hill Farm,
where I started work. The house has now been demolished.
(photo H. J. Mason)

In the observatory
(photo's Ted Eales)

With Sir Peter Scott, in the car park of Welney Wildfowl refuge
(photo Philippa Scott)

6. Tractor Driving

While I was working for father my older brother, Bert, was a tractor driver. During the summer I spent some of my spare time with him as I wanted to learn to drive because I thought it would enable me to earn more money than plover catching. Bert was pleased to let me drive while he had a break, either to eat or just to stretch his legs. He worked for Pat Sullivan who was a contractor. Most of the work was paid for by the acre and most days the tractor hardly stopped as the only way the business could be made to pay was to get over as much land as possible. If I did not go to help him, Bert often ate his food while continuing to work. The tractors, without cabs, gave very little protection from the weather. On cold or wet days he liked to get off periodically, to walk around to try to get his circulation going again or dry out a little if there had been any rain.

After about two years working for father I heard that a Welney farmer was looking for a tractor driver. I decided to go and see the foreman and was given the job. I remember my first day was spent driving an International Farmall 10/12 pulling a binder. There were very few tractors about in those days but farmers who had them, used them for ploughing and cutting the corn. Both tasks were unpopular with horse-keepers as they were hard work for the horses. At harvest time horses had to work long hours to keep the binders going whenever the weather was suitable. They worked through the hottest part of the day and were subjected to the torment of innumerable flies. Small wonder, therefore, that the work was mechanised at the first opportunity.

After harvest, I spent most of the autumn shallow ploughing or "tilting" stubble with a three-furrow Cockshutt plough. This was a traditional autumn cultivation in the area designed to break land about three inches deep to encourage weed seeds to germinate. On our peaty soils this was followed by profuse growth which was ploughed in later. The second ploughing had to be deeper to bury all the stubble and weeds.

I was never happy working on this farm. I was particularly irritated if, when I had ploughing to do, I was brought back to the farm to help load coomb sacks of wheat or barley on to a lorry when there seemed to be plenty of men around the yard who could have done it. On one such occasion I asked for my cards and left at the end of the week.

I was not out of work long as my brother got me a job with his employer, Pat Sullivan. As I was now working for a contractor I had to be prepared to travel to various places, according to where the work was at the time. If the distance was short as, for instance, to Three Holes, Fridaybridge or the Wisbech area, I cycled. The furthest I ever cycled was to a farm near Peterborough, a distance of 20 miles, and as I had to be on the tractor at 7 o'clock I had to leave home soon after 5.30 a.m. When work stopped at 4 p.m. I had to cycle home again. Usually, for long distances, Pat took me in his van, but even so I sometimes had to cycle home in the evening.

Driving these early tractors was hard work. None that I drove before the war had a self-starter. The usual system was to have a petrol/paraffin engine, which was started on petrol and then when it was hot enough it was switched over to paraffin which was much cheaper. There was no such thing as a cab—the driver was exposed to all weathers. One day, perhaps you would be covered in dust, another, soaked to the skin in a sudden storm and another, so cold that when you got off the tractor you could hardly feel your feet or hands.

In addition to the physical discomforts, I had to work for long hours when too much work had been contracted. The marathon which I remember was when I commenced work at midnight on Sunday and worked through non-stop until 4 p.m. on Tuesday. My food was brought by either the farmer or Pat Sullivan, who also made sure that I did not run out of fuel.

I enjoyed working for him and was quite friendly with him and his wife. When working near his house I was often asked in for breakfast or a break during the day. The happy relationship which we had was suddenly interrupted when war was declared on Sunday, 3rd September, 1939. When the family gathered round the radio to hear Mr. Chamberlain make his announcement, none of us could possibly have realised how seriously our lives and way of life would be changed.

The next morning another employee, Ron Smart, and I arrived as usual ready to start work at 7 a.m. Pat, who had reacted immediately to the news, greeted Ron with "Now that war has broken out there will not be much work to do so I shall have to get rid of you. I can't see how I shall find work to keep you both fully employed."

Thinking this was harsh and unjustified I said, "If Ron goes, I'll go." Sharp words followed with the result that we both left on the spot.

Mobilisation of the Territorial Army had occurred much earlier and recruiting for the armed forces was the popular topic of conversation in the village at the time. It was not surprising, therefore, that we decided to join the army. We went straight back to Welney village to catch the 9 o'clock bus to Ely. The recruiting station was a hive of activity as young men queued up to wait their turn to sign on. Unfortunately, Ron was under age by six months and was not accepted. I said "If you won't take him you don't take me" and we left the station together.

So for a period of about six months I did not have regular employment. Plover catching was unprofitable so I did casual work until I was called up for the army. After being a tractor driver for a few years it seemed strange to be back doing odd jobs, working with a gang instead of being on my own. Already there was talk of food shortages because of shipping blockades and other effects of the war. Some men had gone into the army and every available pair of hands was needed to harvest crops so I had no difficulty in finding work.

One Thursday, during the autumn, I went by bus to Ely market with my cousin, Bill Scott. In his early days he was a professional cyclist and skater. On three occasions he was runner-up to the winner, Don Pearson, in the professional skating championships.

Bill had acquired some more land to go with his existing small farm and was considering buying a tractor. We went to Standen's of Ely to look at a John Deere Model B. It seemed this would be ideal for him and a demonstration on his farm was arranged.

As I was the only person who could drive he asked me to try it out. He wanted it for ploughing and row crop work. As I thought it was satisfactory for both, Bill decided to buy it and asked me to spend a few days teaching his son, Reggie, to drive. Reggie was also a professional skater and won the professional championship in 1947.

In those days, workers employed regularly on farms were exempt from call-up but although I knew this, I continued to do casual work. My calling-up papers arrived in early December instructing me to report to Aldershot on 15th December.

7. In the Army

I viewed joining the Army with a mixture of excitement and apprehension but for my parents there was just worry. It was difficult for me, as a young man, to realise how my parents, with their memories of the First World War, must have felt as they with my uncles, aunts, brothers and sisters waved me goodbye.

About 18 months before this, I bought a Raleigh 3-speed hub-dynamo bicycle on hire purchase from Bill Mortram, the local blacksmith, who was a cycle agent. I was still paying 2/6d a week for it but Bill said I need not worry and could finish paying for it later. It was still in immaculate, almost new condition when I left on it for Littleport station on that frosty December morning.

My brother had agreed to pick it up for me from the Railway Tavern where I left it, having paid the landlord 6d. Someone must have known I was leaving for before Captain arrived that evening it had been stolen and was never recovered.

At Aldershot, Army trucks were waiting to take all the new recruits to the barracks. We were allocated to huts and then told to report to the cookhouse. Here we were given a tin plate, knife, fork and spoon and tin dixie but the prospects of drinking from it made me think that the army was obviously not going to be 'home from home' as the recruiting posters promised.

The first difficulty arose the next morning when I was expected to use the dixie for porridge then swill it out ready for a drink of tea. Fortunately, I did not like the porridge so the problem did not arise again.

After breakfast we formed up in squads to march, still in civvies, to the quartermaster's stores to be issued with uniforms. By 9.30 a.m. we had been fully kitted and were on the parade ground in our new uniforms. The sergeant had a loud commanding voice which intimidated many of us. He had us drilling for about half an hour, then said we could fall out for a rest and a cigarette. During this period he came up to me and bellowed "What's your name?"

"Scott" I said.

"Scott, *Sergeant*" he bellowed again, "Stand up and pull your shoulders back. I did the best I could but this did not satisfy him.

"Sit down" he said, and then putting his knee between my shoulders got hold of my arms and tried to heave them back but to no avail. After he realised I had been trying he seemed to take pity on me saying "Do your best lad" and from then on he was much more friendly towards me.

The first week was spent mainly on the parade ground performing simple drill manoeuvres and generally making us familiar with army routine and discipline. At times, there were up to 15 squads drilling on the square which meant that everyone had to be very alert to make sure that the correct order was being obeyed.

A few days before Christmas the squad was sent for dental examination. I was to have three extracted and was told to report to the dentist at 10.00 a.m. The dreaded moment came, the first two came out without any difficulty but the third, an eye tooth, defied the dentist's efforts. He tugged and tugged until the sweat was running down my face with the pain he was inflicting.

There were four dentists all working in the same room. First one, then another and finally the third was asked for his opinion. All four clustered round me, conferred, shook their heads and returned to work. My dentist disappeared for about ten minutes when he returned with a doctor who was puzzled but thought that I should have an X-ray.

A few days later, after I had recovered from a rather bad cold, I was admitted to the military hospital to have an operation to remove the offending tooth as the X-ray had shown the presence of a cyst round the roots. The day after the operation the doctor took some tweezers and removed the dressing. It was a thin medicated tape which seemed endless as he pulled yards and yards from the cavity left by the operation. It reminded me of a magician I had once seen, pulling string from his apparently empty mouth.

After a week in hospital, during which I did cookhouse fatigues, to my great delight I found myself home with seven days sick leave.

It was early in the new year and the partially flooded washes were frozen over. In the Fens, as soon as there is ice, skates appear. Even the fact that there was a war on did not stop the skating although there were fewer than usual on the ice.

Ernie Kent suggested that I should have a go and lent me Bill Scott's skates to use for practice. It was exhilarating to be out in the fresh air of the Fens, with ducks and plover flying around, and the army temporarily forgotten. I entered the local championship race but was beaten in my heat by 'Tubby' Sallis who I think eventually finished third in the championships.

After getting back to Aldershot, I was re-mustered with another squad. The one that I had originally been with was already under orders for France. Later, I learnt that the whole squad was killed. My tooth had saved my life.

When the new squad 'passed out' after its initial six weeks training, it was sent to Margate for further training. Although I was to be a driver, most of the time at this camp and also later at Bognor Regis, I worked in the cookhouse. This was not exciting enough for either my sergeant or me. Wanting to be nearer the action we both volunteered for overseas service.

In a few days after our requests had been granted, we were transferred to Northampton to join a company already under orders for service abroad. There was no embarkation leave for volunteers at this time.

The next day I was on board the Royal Mail 'Andes' which had been converted into a troop ship and was lying in Liverpool docks. We set sail about noon on a calm sea. Fatigued by travelling and little sleep, I found a quiet corner on deck and drifted off to sleep. About three hours later when I woke up the ship was rolling in a rough sea making me sea sick, from which I did not recover for four days.

It took us about a month to reach the coast of Sierra Leone where we made a refuelling stop. Fuel had to be brought out in tugs as our ship was too big for the harbour. We had hardly dropped anchor before we were surrounded by native canoes. Some of the natives brought bananas and oranges for sale, which we purchased by lowering money wrapped in a piece of cloth down to the canoe. A half dozen bananas or a few oranges were tied on in exchange and hauled up. Some of the smaller boys earned money by diving into the sea to catch coins wrapped in silver paper which we threw over for them. Miraculously, they seemed to recover the coins, bringing them up in their mouths, although how deep they had to dive sometimes, we did not really know.

After refuelling, the convoy of eight ships, including the Empress of Britain, the Empress of Canada and the Orcades, set sail for Durban with an escort of a destroyer and cruiser.

At Durban we were allowed four days leave. At first the South Africans showered us with hospitality, collecting us from the quayside and showing us the town before taking us home for the evening. But riots broke out between Merchant Navy men and some Commonwealth troops, a club was wrecked, two soldiers were killed and two drowned, and we were no longer welcome in the port.

On Christmas Day, 1940, we were sailing up the Red Sea to eventually dock at Port Suez. All the troops were taken down the canal to disembark at Port Said. Then the drivers had to return to Port Suez to collect the lorries which had been unloaded there.

Our camp, which was not far from Cairo, was struck by a sandstorm two days after we arrived. I had experienced dust storms in the Fens but they were nothing compared with these Egyptian storms. There was sand everywhere and we were virtually confined to our tents while it lasted.

I was lucky to have three days' leave and managed to look around Cairo and visit the Pyramids during that time.

At camp, the remaining drivers had been sent to Badi to bring back captured Italian lorries and were still away when I returned from Cairo. I found the air buzzing with rumours on the proposed formation of the 8th Army, and endless ideas on our next destination.

Two days later we received orders to be ready to move at dawn on the following day to Alexandria. Ships were docked in readiness for us to drive our lorries on, while all the troops were ordered to muster on the parade ground. The C.O. addressed us and I remember him saying "You are about to embark on a very rough mission from which many of you will not come back. It's a tough job. Good luck to you all."

We marched on to the waiting naval ships and it was not long before we set sail. Although the sea was very rough it no longer upset me. I lay down on one of the lower decks to have a sleep not noticing that I was near an open port hole. I woke up an hour or so later, soaked to the skin and as all the spare kit had been left in the lorries I was unable to change into dry clothes.

Fortunately, a sailor saw me, realised my predicament and took me to the engine room. In less than half an hour I had my clothes dried and on again. For this kindness and later a tot of rum from the ship's ration which the crew gave to us soldiers, I was more than grateful. We were on board H.M.S. Gloucester which was sunk a few months later.

We landed at Pireaus and marched through the streets of Athens. We were the first troops the Greeks had seen in shorts, issued for use in the desert. They gave us an ecstatic welcome with unlimited wine and food. The strength of the wine was too much for most of us and we were drunk long before nightfall. That night I slept on top of three tons of ammunition with which my lorry was loaded.

Our task was to take supplies to the King's Royal Rifles and the Tank Corps, which were hard pressed in the north of Greece. We moved forward in small convoys of three or four lorries supported by a bren gun carrier and an anti-tank gun mounted on one of the lorries. We did our best to keep the supplies moving but the Germans were gradually gaining ground and we progressively retreated until we reached what we soon named 'The Valley of Death'.

With Corporal Baldwin, I volunteered for a supply run to the front. As we were unloading, we could see the enemy's tanks on the ridge in front of us relentlessly pushing forward.

Back in the valley we camouflaged our lorry and equipment with nets and branches but even as we did so a look-out spotted a reconnaissance plane coming out of the sun, swooping down the valley. We all felt sure that in spite of our efforts we would be seen. Just as we were sitting down to have some food, from low down in the valley we heard a siren and I went for shelter behind a boulder. Corporal Baldwin said he was not going to be put off his meal so remained where he was.

It was not long before the screech of about 25 Stuka dive-bombers coming down from a great height filled the valley. They dropped incendiaries, high explosives and strafed us as they went. After repeated flights up and down the valley they departed, leaving us to count our losses.

All the serviceable lorries were assembled ready for a further retreat down the valley. Ambulances collected the wounded and there was the pitiful task of burying the dead, which included my friend of the morning's trip, Corporal Baldwin.

We moved down the narrow tortuous mountain road at night in convoy, using very dim lights. As we were retreating it became obvious to us that the aim must be to evacuate as many troops and as much equipment as possible. Eventually, fuel began to run short and some of the vehicles had to be abandoned. It was decided that there should be one lorry for every 25 men, the rest would have to be destroyed. The easiest and most effective way was to drain the radiators and sumps and run the engine until it seized up. In any event, the lorries could not be driven over the edges of the roads as they might then be spotted by reconnaissance aircraft, letting the enemy know where we were and also revealing our strategy.

When we reached the harbour we could see the ship which had been sent to rescue us in flames just off shore. Revised orders instructed us to proceed as fast as possible to the beaches at Calamata in the far south of Greece. There we were to be taken off by battleship.

We arrived at mid-day and hid in an olive grove two or three miles from the beach until nightfall. In single file we crept through the grove along narrow tracks used by donkeys in normal times. As we got nearer to the beach we met other troops coming back. They told us the ships were leaving but could not offer any explanation. At first I could just see warships outlined against the darkening sky and as they faded into the night I just could not believe what was happening.

We returned to our hiding place from where, the following afternoon we saw a German jeep coming down the road with a white flag flying. Our Brigadier, who was with the German Commander, later told us he had surrendered and that we should lay down our arms. Determined not to give my rifle away I crawled through the undergrowth to a cottage and threw it down a well.

Eventually, all the allied troops were rounded up and taken down to the beach. There were about 10,000 of us assembled there. With the tide coming in and surrounded by German machine guns, for a while I feared we should all be shot and left for the sea to take us away.

It was not until after the war that we learnt the reason for the navy's hurried departure. The Italian Navy was approaching and our ships had to get away from the shallow waters of the bay to be able to manoeuvre to engage the enemy.

Thus on the 24th April, 1941 for us the fight was over and for the rest of the war I was a prisoner.

THE BATTLE OF CALAMATA

29th April, 1941.

There's an old Greek barracks on the flat above the town,
Surrounded by snow-capped mountains which cast shadows down
Onto a huge concourse of men whose names it does not matter;
Thousands of unfortunates captured at Calamata.
They are men of many nations and men of every creed,
Who served their mother country at her greatest hour of need.
For them the fight is over, for them the shouting done,
Their thoughts are for their loved ones from dawn to setting sun.
Their comforts are so very few and sickness fairly rife
To get their few poor meals and watch their health is now their daily life.
Such things are the penalties for prisoners of war
So they are not moaning of events which have gone before
But there is just one thing which rankles in their minds
Why on that fateful night they were all left behind.
The warships stood offshore, monsters of Britain's might
They took a boatload of wounded off and sailed into the night
They do not doubt the reasons which one day they will know
Why they were left upon the beach to be captured by the foe.
There is just one other reason which they would like to hear
Why men died that night to keep those beaches clear
So have a reason England to tell on their release
Until then they can take it, so roll on day of peace.

8. Prisoner of War

After what seemed hours standing around on the crowded beach, we were
lined up in preparation for a march which took us from one end of Greece
to the other, and eventually to Austria. Mostly by day, bedraggled and
demoralised, we marched along the dusty roads, getting food and drink
only when we passed through a village or a town. Then the guards just
went into any cafe and at gun point ordered the proprietor to give us
whatever was available. Sometimes we were herded into railway trucks
and taken as far as possible. Usually we were unloaded and set to march
again because the railway track had been blown up or a bridge destroyed.
At night we slept by the roadside.

Whenever we were unloaded from the trucks we were met by new guards
who arrived on motor cycles with sidecars, or on horseback. As we
trudged along they moved backwards and forwards along the line trying to
keep us together and of course making sure that nobody tried to escape.

At times it was cold, especially at night, but I was fortunate in having my
driver's leather jerkin and my khaki drill. The guards made fires for
themselves and we could hear them talking long into the night as we tried
to sleep on the hard and damp ground.

If we stopped near a stream we could have a wash and remove some of
the dust from our faces but it was impossible to keep clean. During the
march I realised that I was lousy. There is little doubt that I had picked up
the lice in the dirty hovel in which I hid on the night before we surrendered.

When we arrived at Belgrade station, each truck load was allowed five minutes in which to wash, use the toilet and receive a ration of food. This consisted of a one-pound tin of meat and half a loaf of black bread between four of us. We were also given five Yugoslavian cigarettes. These were very strong and after smoking one I found my head going round and round and could not smoke any more of them.

We travelled in the cattle trucks to Marburg, which is very close to the Austrian border. During the journey we passed through mile after mile of marshy swamp, which I have since been told is a wonderful place for birds.

At Marburg we were taken to a Prisoner of War camp where there were already hundreds of Russian prisoners. Here I met my friend Fred Leeford from Little Downham, near Ely, with whom I spent a good deal of the time. When we were not queueing up for food we were speculating on what would happen to us.

One day a notice appeared on the orders board "Men wanted for farm work. Put your POW number here". Fred and I went to read it and as we stood discussing it somebody who had overheard our conversation said "Do you come from Norfolk bor?" "Why yes, tha' I do" I replied, pleased to hear a friendly voice in my own dialect.

Bill Adcock, who came from near Norwich, had asked the question. He had with him Jack Canham, who also came from Norfolk. All four of us became pals and fell into animated conversation trying to find out as much as we could about each other and the places which we knew at home.

The request for farm workers received no response so after several days the camp commandant ordered the guards to get us on to the parade ground. He shouted at us "I have 10,000 prisoners in this camp, when I want twenty for work, not one comes forward. There will be no more food or water until I get the men I want."

For two days we starved. The pangs of hunger gradually began to be felt. Eventually, Jack, Bill and I decided that we must try to survive and it was only after careful thought and with grave misgivings that we put our numbers up on the board. Others joined us and by the end of the day there were twenty numbers on the board.

Next morning we were called to the guard room and marched away to the call of "Nazi's" and "You'll be sent to the salt mines" and "It's only a fiddle, you'll never be sent to a farm." The fear of the unknown future we faced was deepened by these calls but there was no going back.

I was one of a group of twelve who were each issued with an army blanket, half a loaf of bread and a German sausage before being marched to the railway station, which we reached at about 7 a.m. We were eyed with curiosity by the natives and felt very conspicuous in our P.O.W's dress with our numbers stitched across the breast. I still remember mine was 8192 KGF.

We were taken to Graz. From the station we went by tram as far as the line went. Then were marched down a mule track which was a short cut to a state farm. We entered the farmyard through a brick archway and were taken to a long building which was to be our billet.

44

Having had little food for weeks I had learned to use any that I was given sparingly and still had half my bread and sausage left expecting that it would have to last me until at least the next morning. I was therefore very surprised to find that a meal had been prepared. It consisted of soup, salad with lettuce, tomato and cucumber and bread. There was no butter but there was some rape oil for dressing the salad. This was the first decent meal I had eaten for about three months and even now I can remember how wonderful it tasted.

Our billet was spartan but better than at the transit camp. On the iron beds we had palliasses and pillow cases which we filled with oat straw. We were issued with another two blankets and had the benefit of an old cooking range in which we could light a fire.

Before being locked in for the night we were taken for a walk round the farm to see the cattle and crops. Reveille was at 6 a.m. For breakfast we were taken to a large mess hall where all the workers had their meals. In the centre of a long table was a bowl of meal which, I learned later, was made from maize, ground to about the size of rice and then boiled for 20 minutes. We were each given a bowl of coffee and a spoon but until the workers started to eat, we sat there wondering what to do next.

The method was to take a spoonful of meal from the communal bowl, dip it into the coffee and eat it. I never got used to this way of eating, nor to the garlic in the food at other meals and was glad when eventually we got permission to cater for ourselves in our billet.

After breakfast, the foreman lined us up and marched us off to the market gardening area where we set to digging, using long-handled spades. Although I had never used this implement before I soon got used to it and found the work very easy. Jack Canham, who had done farm work before the war, also found it easy and we found we had to work very slowly so as not to get ahead of the others, who were finding it difficult.

We were allowed a break about 9 a.m. and were given a jug of raw cider. This was made on the farm as there were plenty of apples available.

During the morning the foreman came round. He soon realised from the neat appearance of my digging that I must have been used to farm work. He took me to one side and began to make hand movements which I interpreted as asking me if I knew how to milk. At first I pretended not to understand and then I realised that if I milked, I would be able to steal milk for all of us. I asked Jack if he could milk and when he said he could, we both agreed to help in the cowshed.

We were taken to see the cows tied up in the shed. Each had a number tag and a small notice board in front of it on which the milk yield and fat percentage were recorded.

After a few days digging we were sent to help with haymaking. Jack and I were each given scythes to help mow where the machine could not reach, while the rest of our squad helped the women to turn the swathes with wooden forks. Work ceased about 7 p.m. when the dew began to fall and make the hay damp. All the hay was put into big heaps or cocks overnight in case of rain. In the morning, if it needed further drying, it was thrown out again but if it was fit, it was carted into the barn.

45

When heavy clouds gathered over the mountains the natives knew that there would be a thunderstorm later in the day. Then as much of the hay as possible was carted and the remainder put into cocks.

For carting, they used long low trailers with raves or ladders at each end but no sides. One trailer was drawn by two oxen, and each of the others by a pair of horses. There were no young able-bodied men on the farm as they were in the army. Consequently, Jack and I were given the hardest work of pitching the hay on to the trailer. We soon found that we could lift a whole cock at a time and it required three of the old men to load while we were pitching.

Although the farming methods were primitive in many ways, there were a few very advanced techniques used. When unloading the hay, for instance, there was no hand labour needed. The whole load was lifted by an electrically operated grab and taken along a rail into the hay loft above the cows.

After the haymaking was finished Jack and I were sent to help with the cows. We had to be in the cowshed by 2.30 a.m., which meant that the guard had to get up and let us out of the billets. The guards were soldiers who had fought on the Russian front. They were given a period of this type of duty to recuperate before returning to the front line. We were very unpopular when we became milkers because the guards resented having to get up in the middle of the night.

The first morning I was introduced to a ritual which was to follow twice daily for the next two years. Having been given a clean smock, the head milker came up and showed me how to strap the milking stool round my waist. This done, I was told to wash my hands and stand at the back of the shed. The stool, which was now firmly fixed to me, had only one leg and as I stood there I wondered just how difficult it would be to balance on it.

Promptly at 3 a.m. the signal to start was given. I was given twelve cows to milk. It was some years since I had last milked. My wrists began to ache, then to hurt, but somehow I got them all done. There was a little relief after finishing each cow as the milk had to be taken to be weighed and recorded before it was tipped into a churn. After a few days the pain in my wrists disappeared as my muscles became accustomed again to milking and I was able to make the froth spill over from the pail as I got into the rhythm.

The milk which I was able to get from the dairy was very useful as we were, by this time, catering for ourselves. The food we were given was sparse and unpalatable. We would have had a struggle to survive had it not been for the food parcels which we received weekly.

Our weekly rations consisted of a 2-kilo loaf of bread, about two ounces of butter, a spoonful of jam and sometimes a little meal. The contents of the Red Cross parcels varied according to their country of origin. The ones we received came from either England, Scotland or Canada. I particularly remember that the Canadian parcels contained coffee, which the Austrians found very difficult to obtain. They would exchange almost

46

anything for this so we were able to get flour (barley), eggs and other fresh commodities from them. Some of the parcels contained a powdered milk called Klim which proved extremely useful after we stopped milking and could no longer get fresh milk.

I still have some of the recipes we used and typical examples of these are:-

Fig Pudding:

Ingredients: figs, currants, raisins, stale bread.

Method: Stew figs and currants in plenty of water so that there is enough juice to mix breadcrumbs after boiling. Mix the same amount of breadcrumbs as fruit to a good solid dough. It can then be boiled, steamed or baked. Crushed biscuits can be used instead of breadcrumbs.

Biscuit Fingers

Slice dry crusts of bread into fingers. Soak in treacle for 2 or 3 hours and then fry in fat.

My period of milking came to an abrupt end when I nearly cut my finger off. For firewood we used any timber we could get from the forest. One day, when I was using an axe to chop some wood, the handle caught against a branch and I hit my finger instead of the wood. Blood immediately began to flow and seconds later, when I saw the lower part of my finger hanging down, I thought I had severed it completely.

An Australian prisoner called Bill came running to me after he heard my shriek, followed by "Cor blast, I've cut my finger off." He helped me to stagger across to the office where the clerk called an ambulance and in a state of panic gave me a glass of brandy. He bandaged it as best he could, using lollipop sticks for splints.

The ambulance took me to a German military hospital where I was taken to the operating theatre. As I had been given brandy I could not be given any anaesthetic so was told to look the other way while the surgeon scraped the bone, put the finger together again and stitched it up. I can vividly remember that the nurse who assisted him had a broken arm in a sling but such was the shortage of staff that she had to remain on duty.

I expected to be returned to the farm but to my surprise was kept in hospital for about a month. With the exception of one New Zealand prisoner who had had an appendix operation, all the patients were German soldiers. The majority were being treated for frostbite which they had suffered while serving on the Russian front. As I walked along the ward I could see the pitiful state of some of their frost-bitten legs. The treatment seemed to be to use maggots to eat away the decaying flesh and then, after cleaning out the wound, to carry out skin grafts. Soldiers receiving this treatment could not see what was going on as a screen was placed across the centre of the bed.

When I returned to the farm I was given the small female cattle to look after. All the steer calves were sent at birth to the veal factory. Over the winter the calves got to know me very well and when let out into the nearby pasture were trained to follow me. Each had a chain round the neck but the leader also had a cow-bell.

In the late spring, all the young stock was sent away to the Alps for summer grazing. As the cattle knew me I had to help to get them there. Jack and the head milker also came. We walked them down to Graz station and loaded them into cattle trucks. After about a four-hour journey we arrived at our destination.

We then started the long climb up to the farm which was about 2,500 metres above sea level. I led all the way and the cattle followed on behind. Alongside the track there was a stream. At intervals there was a water trough made from a hollowed-out tree trunk, at which the cattle could drink. All the fences were made from rails with twigs braided into them.

The shepherd, who looked after the cattle during the summer, lived in the mountains all the year round. In the autumn he had to stock up with rations to last over the winter and in some years he was cut off for months by heavy snowfalls. He was very pleased to see us and gave us a good meal. After sleeping overnight in the hay barn we returned the next day, the hardest part of the journey being the walk down the mountain to the railway station. The cattle remained on the Alpine pastures until September when the three of us again made the journey, this time to fetch them back, again.

During the last winter that I was prisoner the weather was extremely cold and I was sent to help cut blocks of ice from the frozen lake. Each morning we set out with the oxen-drawn wagons and our boots well wrapped in sacks. After drilling holes, blocks were cut with an ice saw and then slid up a plank on to the wagon. They were stored in an ice house which was dug out of the hillside. In the summer they were fetched out and sold to the local brewery.

When spring came I was given the job of cultivating with a tractor while Jack used a horse team.

Soon after we arrived at the farm we were able to get a radio from an Austrian for 2,000 cigarettes. It was fairly easy to save such a large number as most months I received 1,000 from my mother and 1,000 from the Isle of Ely Red Cross. The 5-valve set was kept in the hay loft and whenever possible, one of the prisoners listened to the news, making notes so that he could tell everyone else later. Thus we were able to get some idea of the progress of the war.

On the day that we first heard of the allied landings in Europe, we all reported sick, smuggled the radio into our billet, put it under the table with blankets draped over it and spent the day listening to the news.

In the spring of 1945 we noticed the increase in the intensity of air raids. By night we could hear the drone of Lancasters as the RAF went over and by day we saw the tell-tale vapour trails left by squadrons of USAF Liberators and Flying Fortresses.

Sometimes bombs dropped near the farm. We were told that during air raids we were to look after the women and children. One afternoon a string of bombs fell across some smallholdings near where Jack and I were working. We saw smoke coming from a demolished house and as we approached it we passed a large hole, already filling with water, which obviously contained an unexploded bomb. We realised that we had to evacuate the area as quickly as possible.

We found one old man in a dazed condition near the demolished house. Frantic signals told us there was someone in there so we went to look. We found his daughter lying flat on her back with severe injuries, including a broken leg. Using a door as a stretcher, we managed to get her out.

More frantic signals from both father and daughter sent us back into the ruins to look for her two year old son. We eventually found him but a beam had fallen across him and he must have been killed instantly. We pacified her as best we could and using straw as bedding made her comfortable in the horse-drawn wagon to take her to hospital. By this time there were no motor ambulances available in the area.

She insisted that Jack and I went with her and eventually we were allowed to carry her into the hospital's operating theatre. She recovered and returned home about three days before we left the farm.

About this time there was another incident which remains in my memory. One of the old Austrians was working with a pair of horses rolling some land in preparation for drilling. He had with him a grandson who, foolishly, he allowed to ride on the shafts. The boy fell off and before the horses stopped, the roller, which was spiked, had gone over him. The old man's scream for help was heard by Bill, who was hoeing potatoes nearby. He ran over to help, lifted the roller and freed the boy. He then ran with him in his arms for about half a mile back to the farm. I shall never know how he managed to lift that roller for later three of us tried unsuccessfully to do so.

From listening to the radio we knew that the war must be coming to an end. We were therefore not surprised to be told by the German guards that the Russians were advancing towards the area and that we could stay or go, whichever we chose.

We unanimously decided to go, making Switzerland our objective. We piled our few belongings and what food we could get on to an old handcart and set off on what was to be a 6-week trek, ending in Salzburg. During this time we were unable to have a wash or shave and had no idea what was happening with regard to the war as our radio was a mains set and had to be left behind.

A German guard accompanied us. The main problem was food. We stole chickens and vegetables whenever possible. One day we were passing a field where the farmer was planting potatoes. The guard told us to get some and while the workers were dropping seed at one end of the field, we were picking it up at the other.

Our journey ended at a concentration camp near Salzburg. Here we persuaded a guard to let us go through a hole in the fence to get a calf from a nearby farm. I knocked on the farmhouse door and while I distracted the farmer by "talking" to him in sign language, the rest of the gang killed a calf and dragged it back to the billet.

We lit a fire in the room, skinned and jointed the calf and stewed it in an old tin bath.

The next day we could hear the distant sound of gunfire. That night during the hours of darkness, all the German guards disappeared. We awoke to freedom and set off down the main road in the direction of Salzburg which we could just see in the distance. In the town there were banners across the streets proclaiming "Welcome to our liberators."

We walked on until we met a convoy of American soldiers. After friendly greetings they rounded us all up and took us back to the concentration camp. Everyone was interrogated and asked to give name, number, rank, unit and other relevant details. The commander told us that we would be flown home as soon as possible and that within 48 hours of landing in England would be back with our families.

While waiting for a flight we were allowed out into the town from 9 a.m. to 9 p.m. Food, mainly sweet corn and fried chicken, was served from a mobile canteen. Few of us really enjoyed these first few days of freedom as the thought uppermost in our minds was getting home.

I shall never forget the day I returned to this country after the war ended. The troop plane took off from Salzburg at 9 a.m. and landed at Guildford at 1 p.m. All the ex-prisoners were taken to Haywards Heath where we were first given a routine de-lousing treatment of powder (probably based on DDT) blown up our trouser legs and into our jacket sleeves. The camp was festooned with flags, bunting and "Welcome Home" signs.

In the mess room the trestle tables were loaded with all kinds of food and for the first time in four years I was able to enjoy a really good English meal.

After we had been sorted out into our respective units we were taken over to a Nissen hut in which there were 25 beds already prepared for our arrival. On each bed was a telegram on which was already typed "Arrived home .... see you soon" and all we had to do was to fill in the name and address of our next of kin. It says something for the efficiency of the postal service in those days for my mother and father received my telegram between 3 and 4 o'clock that afternoon.

We were then taken to another hut where we stripped off our clothes and told we could keep them if we liked but if not, they would be burnt. Then after having a bath and shave, followed by a medical examination, we were issued with new uniforms. Members of the Women's Voluntary Service were there to sew on any insignia and badges and also to make any necessary alterations.

We stayed overnight, were issued with new kit, given double ration cards and a leave pass for six weeks, together with six weeks' pay, before being taken to Liverpool Street station. There was only one train to Ely that night, which arrived at 1 o'clock on the Sunday morning.

Ely station was dark and almost deserted when I alighted from the train with my kit bag and I wondered how I would manage to get to Welney. As I walked down the platform I saw a man who asked me where I was going. He had come to pick somebody up for Downham Market but as his passenger failed to arrive he very kindly took me home.

My parents had not really expected me to arrive that night but they had put the "Welcome Home" notice across the path and the door was not locked.

They were naturally overjoyed to have me home and soon had my younger brothers running down the road to let relations know that I had returned.

By 6 a.m. most of the family had gathered together and it was decided that we should all go down to the Crown to see Saul Malkin. He had written to me once a month all through the war and had repeatedly said he would have a bottle of whisky ready for when I got back.

I knocked on the door and shouted through the letter box "It's Josh." He was soon on his way down the stairs but without stopping to open the door went straight down to the cellar to get the whisky.

My joy at being home was complete when I had my first breakfast of bacon and eggs for nearly five years.

9. Shepherd of the Washes

My father had continued to look after about 150 acres of washes throughout the war but he gladly handed them over to me when I was demobbed in February 1946. It was over six years since I had last worked on them and it was wonderful to be back. In the first six weeks I strolled over the fields, making sure the gates and watering places were ready for the cattle. As the spring came, the migratory ducks and swans left but the skylarks and plovers were joined by the summer visitors which nest in the area.

Early in the spring the first cattle arrived, together with a few mares which were not required for working on their owners' farms. Soon after their arrival I had to visit the doctor as I had developed a cyst on the side of my face. It did not seem at all serious to me but I was sent to see an RAF doctor at The Grange, Littleport (now the T.G.W.U. convalescent home) and he admitted me to the RAF Hospital at Ely.

Shortly after returning to Welney I met Olive and we had become very attached to each other. She cycled from Littleport to Ely each day to visit me, which was very comforting as at first my condition deteriorated. However, eventually I recovered and one day as we walked round the hospital garden during my convalescence, I asked her to marry me. I was delighted when she accepted and we agreed that the wedding should take place on Boxing Day.

It was not long before I realised that I could not earn a living from the washes alone. Spring was a busy time on the farms so I was able to obtain casual work with my cousin and other small farmers.

My daily routine was to get up early enough to cycle round the washes to look at all the cattle and horses. When a quick check showed that all the animals were grazing or resting, I could go off to my daytime work. But if there was an animal missing I had to walk round until I found it. Perhaps it was just hidden by some tall grass, nevertheless I had to be sure it was not ill or stuck in a ditch somewhere.

Field work on the farms stopped at 4 p.m. when I went home, had my tea and then repeated my morning round to check the animals again.

During the late summer, when there was less to do on the farms, I worked full-time on the washes. Most days I mowed thistles and pulled ragweed where necessary. As this was not part of the normal shepherding work, I was paid extra for doing it, usually on a piece-work rate at so much for an acre or for the field.

Being on the washes all day was ideal at this time of the year as I could watch the plover which I would be netting and also keep my eye on any ducks or pheasants that were about.

Plover netting was permissible from 1st September to the end of February at that time. At the end of August I started to flood about five acres of wash, just as my father and grandfather had done before me. Water was let in from the tidal (Hundred Foot) river until it flooded the whole field, except for a small area where I was to set up my plover netting bed.

Most of the washes were grazed by the owners' cattle and there was therefore no restriction on how long they could be left to graze. Consequently, some of them did not go away until just before Christmas.

In spite of having the cattle I was able to spend several days each week in catching plover. The catches were not very good but the price never fell below 2/6d, and rose to 3/3d on occasions.

When the weather grew colder in November, I set my punt gun up on a bank overlooking some fairly deep water. I had a few shots at duck but without any great success. As soon as it began to freeze I had to stop plover netting because the net became frozen into the grass.

To attract ducks I broke a hole in the ice each day. One evening at dusk, as I peered cautiously over the bank, I could see the silhouette of four geese in the fading light. They were splashing in the water and eventually moved so that I could get a reasonable shot at them.

After firing, I raced across the ice and picked up two dead birds, a third one I chased and caught at the edge of the ice but of the fourth there was no sign. Next morning, as soon as it was light, I was down on the washes and found the last bird dead in some reeds in one of the ditches. These four pinkfeet were the only geese I ever shot on the washes.

54

Olive and I were married on Boxing Day, 1947. All the large family had gathered together for Christmas and we prolonged the festivities for another day, much to everyone's enjoyment.

Towards the end of December there was a thaw, enabling me to resume plover netting. One day while I was busy setting my nets I noticed that there was someone on the bank watching me. The same thing happened the following day but I carried on as usual.

Later on the second day I saw Hagen Smart in the 'Lamb and Flag' and told him what had happened. He looked surprised and exclaimed, "Haven't you heard the news then?"

This took me aback and all I could say was "What news?"

"Plovers are protected now and netting is illegal."

This was shattering news for me and since nobody else had mentioned it, I took no notice but returned to my netting the following day.

I sent off a sackful of best quality birds and my worst fears were soon confirmed. The game dealer sent me a cheque in payment but added a note to say that as it was now illegal to offer them for sale, he would be unable to accept any more.

Thus one of my sources of income was swept away. I wrote to the local Member of Parliament, Major Legge-Bourke, who replied by saying that when the bill was debated the majority considered that the plover was a beneficial bird as it consumed harmful snails which were carriers of liver fluke, in addition to eating other pests. There was concern that the population of this species was dropping and it therefore needed the protection of legislation.

I believe that there has been a further decline since netting was stopped. This may be due to many factors but I doubt if the ban on netting has had much effect. In those days most broods of plovers consisted of three or four chicks but in recent years I have not seen a hen with more than two chicks.

In the early days of January, 1947, I managed to do some punt gunning but it was not long before the Fens, like the rest of the country, was held in the iron grip of one of the worst winters in living memory. It was a wonderful time for the old fenland sport of speed skating. There was little else to do except for an odd day or two riddling potatoes. Even then, the solidly frozen earth covering the clamp had to be removed with a pick-axe and the greatest care was needed to make sure the potatoes did not freeze during riddling and that those left were well covered up at the end of the day.

I was glad to earn some money in this way as I now had my wife to provide for.

Everybody knew that the thaw must come eventually but as February drew to a close without any sign of a let-up, nobody realised what devastation was to follow shortly. The thaw started in the second week of March and was accompanied by heavy rainfall.

River levels quickly rose dangerously high but as there was so much ice around the water could not flow freely to the pumps and the sea. Every available person was called upon to walk the banks to see whether any breaches were appearing. A small crack could be successfully stopped by a few sandbags but if water trickled through, it could soon wash the bank away and create a serious breach.

I was working on a section of the Ouse near Littleport and one evening met up with some friends on the main road bridge. Suddenly we realised that something had happened as the river was flowing fast and the level had dropped about twelve inches. Later, I found that this was due to a massive breach in the river wall near Southery, causing extensive flooding in Feltwell Fen.

When I got home that night I was taken ill with tonsilitis and had to stay indoors for six weeks. Although I saw nothing of the flooding, I knew what was happening but even so, I was surprised at the damage done in the washes. Pack ice had been blown from one side of the washes to the other with each shift of the wind. In the process gates, posts and bridges had been swept away.

All had to be replaced before any cattle or horses could be allowed to graze. They were late coming but after a hectic period of putting in posts, hanging gates, replacing bridges and removing the flotsam and jetsam left by the flood water, there was reason to hope for better days ahead.

The weather in the late spring of that year soon merged into summer and it was not long before we were suffering from severe drought conditions. The level of the tidal river began to fall and it became brackish. In a normal year, water can be let in from the river into the ditches which separate the fields in the washes. By midsummer no more could be let in, with the result that water levels in the ditches began to fall and more and more cattle got stuck as they went further into them to drink.

Nearly every day I had two or three bullocks or horses to pull out of the mud. Sometimes I managed on my own but often I had to get somebody to help me. Then, most days when I arrived home, my wife would say "Uncle George is in trouble and needs help."

Uncle George Kent was shepherd of about 500 acres to the south of the Welney road. This is the land which now forms part of that owned by the Royal Society for the Protection of Birds and the Cambridgeshire and Isle of Ely Naturalists' Trust. He had a very busy time that summer as cattle were regularly getting stuck, the worst morning being when there were eight animals all in one ditch.

Most owners took their cattle away early that autumn so I was free to help with some of the corn harvesting and threshing and also do some tractor driving for my cousin. There was plenty of contracting work to do as few of the small farmers had tractors of their own at that time.

On the 1st October, when the pheasant shooting began, I went round the washes and shot enough birds to pay for my game licence and for cartridges for the rest of the season.

I managed to shoot a few duck during morning and evening flights but was not very successful punt gunning until Hagen Smart loaned me his punt and Tommy Rudland gave me his gun called "Jarminy". This was the gun on which I had learned to shoot and I was overjoyed to have the use of it.

Tommy Rudland had given up punt gunning and was making a living from his land. One day he said that if I would help him to riddle some onions and sell them for him he would give me "Jarminy". This I did quite willingly because I knew a dealer who wanted to buy some onions.

"Jarminy" was reputed to be the best gun on the washes. It served me well until one frosty morning when I tried to cock it, the main spring broke. Later I was told that the metal was probably more brittle because of the very low temperature.

Local enquiries for a new spring were unsuccessful until I consulted a gunsmith in a nearby town. He said that he could get one made at Birmingham but it would be very expensive. He knew that I was very short of money and yet had to get the gun repaired because my winter livelihood partly depended upon it.

Then he made me an offer, "I'll get the new spring if you will give me that Westley Richards muzzle loader that you have got." This was a double-barrel 12-bore which could be broken down and fitted into a case together with the ram rod, powder flask and shot measurer. I was very proud of this gun and did not want to part with it but felt that I must get the punt gun mended. I reluctantly agreed to his offer and received the new spring about a fortnight later.

It was years later that I realised the true value of the 12-bore and what a fool I had been.

During the early part of 1950 I was helping a cousin, who was a builder, to modernise the cottage where my parents lived when most of their children were born, when I received a message that Hagen Smart wanted to see me. In the evening I got on my old motor cycle—a recent acquisition —and went along to Norway House to see him.

Hagen was the grandson of the famous Welney skater, James Smart, who won the professional championship of Great Britain in 1889, 1890 and 1895. He went on to win the world championship and skated in Holland, Germany and Norway. While in Norway he met a manufacturer of skates called Harold Hagen. These skates were so good that James became agent for them in this country and on the profits he made, was able to build Norway House. His son, Harold Hagen Smart, was named after his business associate.

I had known Hagen all my life as he was shepherd of the washes which adjoined my father's and like me, he had taken over from his father.

He answered my knock and took me into his living room. After we were seated, he turned to me and said "have you any idea why I've sent for you?" To this I could truthfully reply that I had not.

He went on to explain that he was a sick man and although he was only 62, he would be forced to retire. "I've recommended you to the owners of my washes and all are agreed that they would like you to take over from me. Can you do it?" he asked.

I knew that he was shepherd on 400-500 acres and if I could take them over my livelihood would be assured. However, I had a baby daughter as well as my wife to think about. Money was short and I realised that I could not possibly manage until the end of the grazing season when the shepherd is normally paid.

When I mentioned this to Hagen, he proved what a good friend he was. He had already thought that this would be a problem and offered me some money in advance for looking after the washes he owned and promised to help me until I was paid.

On the way home I called in at the Three Tuns and had my usual pint of beer. I sat with some of the regulars, only half listening to their conversations while I thought about my new responsibilities. I got to thinking of Hagen and some of the tales he had told me about his father.

I remembered he had said that on autumn or winter afternoons his father would cross the Old Bedford river in a little boat moored near Norway House, taking some freshly cut willow sticks with him. He would stick one in the bank where he landed, another about half a mile upstream and a third about half a mile downstream. In the morning, he and Hagen went over to see if any had been gnawed by a hare during the night. If one of the sticks was displaying a white patch where the bark had been stripped off, Hagen was sent to walk near the river to beyond where the hare was thought to be. Then he returned along the bank towards his father, who stood ready to shoot if a hare was disturbed and driven towards him. I suppose this little strategy saved time, as long walks across the washes were thus avoided.

James Smart had a way with catching eels. If a sheep died at the right time of the year, he cut its stomach open, weighted it with bricks and then tied a rope round one of its legs before throwing it into the river. Early next morning, just as dawn was breaking, he hauled it out. Usually its stomach was full of eels and the family kept some for their own use, the remainder being sold. It was possible to catch eels for a week or more in this way.

For a time, Hagen and his father shepherded adjoining washes. One morning when Hagen was doing his rounds, he discovered a big horse in a ditch. Using blocks and pulleys, and with his father's help, he tried to pull it out but it was a jibber and would not help itself.

After struggling for a time, James said, "I've had enough of this, I know a way to shift it."

Hagen was told to hold the ropes and be prepared to heave when the horse began to struggle. James meanwhile picked up an umbrella which he had brought with him just in case it was needed. He got down into the ditch as near to the horse's head as possible and opened and shut the umbrella as sharply as he could two or three times. The horse was so frightened that it reared up thus enabling Hagen to pull it clear.

I was roused from my thoughts by someone saying, "You're very quiet tonight Josh, h've you got something worryin' you?"

"That I have." I said as I walked out of the bar. Apart from thinking about the extra work, I knew that other shepherds would want to take over from Hagen and there would be a lot of criticism when the news broke.

I managed fairly well that year as I found that I could ride over most of my territory on my old motor bike. Looking at the animals was much easier as I could quickly go round each field and when I needed help I could soon go and fetch someone. Early in the next year when George Kent was taken ill and told to take a complete rest, another uncle, Will Kent, and I, agreed that we would look after his washes for him. The idea was that each day Will would start at one end of George's area and I would work from the other end until we met somewhere in the middle. I thought it would not take me long on my bike to look after some of his washes as well as my own.

At the time, some new houses were being built at Welney and two of the Irish workers were lodging at the Crown. They were gamblers and following a good win they decided to buy a motor bike. Since I rode one they sought my help.

There was one advertised for sale at Littleport so the three of us managed to get a lift there in order to go and see if it was suitable. It was a Triumph 350 c.c. priced at £65. I tried it out and thought it was a good buy. My friends paid for it and it was decided that I should ride it home with Paddy as a passenger, while John would hitch-hike back to Welney.

Coming out of Littleport, Paddy asked me to let him have a go. He had never ridden before so I had to tell him what to do. We turned off down Black Bank where there is a long straight stretch of road and were going well when we were signalled to stop by a police car coming towards us.

The two policemen were looking for a motor bike being ridden by two men in army uniform as there had been a report of a traffic offence in Ely by a vehicle of this description. Both Paddy and I were wearing army tunics and therefore fitted the description. After explaining we had only come from Littleport, one of the policemen said that we were obviously not the men being sought but for some reason, the other one was not satisfied. He asked Paddy to stop the engine but of course he did not know what to do so I had to stretch forward to move the exhaust lift.

The second policeman immediately realised that something was wrong and asked for our driving licences. When Paddy could not produce one he took our names and addresses and said that we would be hearing from the Court.

In due course, a summons was received and after we explained the circumstances, I was fined 30 shillings and disqualified for 12 months, and Paddy was treated the same, although disqualification was of no consequence to him since he had no licence in any case.

The solicitor was able to help me to get my licence back after six months but in the meantime, I was restricted to riding only on the washes and it was hard work using a bicycle again on the public roads.

In a way, I got my own back on one of the magistrates as I was a shepherd for some of his cattle and horses, and I doubled my charges to him that year.

During these early years as a shepherd I managed to do some wildfowling, sometimes shooting an odd duck or two to eat and sometimes for sale. There was a gradual increase in the number of people who wanted to have an evening or morning flight and whenever I could, I arranged to take a client along as this was additional income.

One of my most regular visitors was Dr. Burnet, who tried to come once or twice each week throughout the season. He frequently brought a friend or two with him, all of whom were good keen shots. At the end of each flight we mostly had a good bag to show for our efforts. One of the regular friends was another doctor who did not shoot but was a keen birdwatcher and enjoyed being out in the washes to see the ducks in flight.

The circle of friends introduced to the washes by the doctor gradually expanded to include specialists from Addenbrooke's hospital, a local industrialist and many others who perhaps only came once or twice while staying in the area.

There is one of this group whom I have always admired as being an outstanding sportsman. He loved the sport so much that no weather was bad enough to keep him away as long as there was the slightest chance of being able to shoot. Fortified by a tot of whisky from his hip flask which he always carried, he was prepared to face any weather. He must have shot more ducks with fewer cartridges than any man on the washes. Others may have been better shots in daylight but he was unsurpassed when there was little light at dusk or dawn. He was always annoyed when he shot a duck or snipe and could not find it, as it was his ambition to pick up everything he shot if it was humanly possible to do so. Even if he had to walk through icy water above his knees, he was not deterred.

One evening, one of the guests was a colonel who was commander of a nearby American air base. We met at the bridge near the end of the track which runs north into the washes.

The track was very muddy and it was therefore with a feeling of relief that I saw the American arrive in a jeep, driven by a major. It was equipped with a gun rack on which we stored our guns and gear. Then followed a hair-raising trip at 25-30 miles per hour, with the jeep slithering and sliding from one side of the track to the other. At times I thought we would all end up in the ditch which ran alongside the track but eventually we arrived without mishap at a small field which was partially flooded. I placed the colonel and major in what were the most promising spots, left the doctor about 50 yards away and then went a further 50 yards before I stopped.

There was not a single flight of ducks near me and I did not once even cock my gun. I took comfort, however, from the regular reports which I could hear coming from the place where the Americans were located. When things had quietened down and it was really too dark to see any more ducks, I made my way back to the doctor who, like me, had not had any shots.

60

The Americans had enjoyed their shooting but had not picked up any of the fallen birds. They had marked them fairly well and with the help of my dog, we soon had them in the bag. In the darkness, I was not sure what species of birds we were picking up but I was to be surprised when I emptied the bag back at the house and found that they were all seagulls! Only then did I realise that I should have explained that we do not shoot seagulls in this country.

The number of wildfowlers increased to such an extent that the area was becoming over-shot during the late 1950s and early 1960s. There was so much disturbance that it was difficult to get more than an odd shot or two during the flightings.

Many of the shooters who were coming regularly to my washes were intelligent, thoughtful and knowledgeable wildfowlers. While they were keen on their sport they did not want to see the wildfowl shot to the extent that they were driven away from the washes or that the survival of the species might be endangered.

Typical of the men and their attitude is the incident when Bruce Hobbs and a friend were lucky enough to be shooting when there was a very good flight of pintail. After shooting three of the birds they decided that was enough and enjoyed the rest of the evening watching the remainder of the flock as they flew round and round before they eventually settled down. Pintails are very nervous when they first come back from migration and take a long time to look round before they feel it is safe to land.

Mr. I. Radclyffe, another keen shot, never shot more than four ducks at a flight but liked to stay to watch after he had got his bag. During a discussion in the Lamb and Flag one evening with a group of such wildfowlers, the suggestion was made that better control of the shooting could be achieved by the formation of a syndicate. The idea was that it should acquire the shooting rights for all the land which I shepherded and that I should look after the shoot and make arrangements for members when they wanted to come down for a morning or evening flight.

The syndicate was eventually formed with Dr. Dosseter, R. Clifton-Brown, Bryn Ford, Bruce Hobbs, Major Hull, I. Radclyffe, T. Reynolds, H. Rosselle, J. Rowley, P. Schwind, J. Smalley and B. Taylor as members.

It was agreed that each member should be limited to six flights each year and this would prevent wildfowl being shot too frequently in the area over which rights were held. In fact, many of the members did not use up their allocation of flights but when they came they could usually be sure of some good sport.

The syndicate has been very successful and is still in existence although all the land over which it originally had shooting rights is now under the control of the Wildfowl Trust.

A complete ban on shooting was agreed by all syndicate members during the severe winter of 1963, when the wildfowl were hard-pressed for food and many perished. That year I had some mallard and wigeon decoys on the washes and had to go over daily to feed them. The Hundred Foot

61

river, which I normally crossed by punt, was filled with huge lumps of pack-ice which flowed to and fro with the tide. It was too dangerous for me to cross in my fragile craft so I had to go round, using my motor bike to ride along the bank.

One day, on the track, I saw a heron which was unable to fly. When I picked it up it grabbed my wrist in its powerful beak. I could only break its iron grip by putting the lower part of its beak under my knee and heaving on the upper part with my free hand. This done, and with a secure hold on its beak, I had a look at it only to realise that it had been standing still so long that its feathers had frozen and its wings were frozen to its body. The warmth from my hands was sufficient to stroke the ice from its feathers and after a while it was able to fly away. To my astonishment it was there again the next day and I had to de-ice its feathers before it could fly. This time it did not attempt to peck me. Over the next four to five weeks it was there on a number of occasions and each time I had to free its wings before it could fly.

After the syndicate had been formed I decided to exchange "Bacca Jack" for some eel hives. These I used for a number of seasons to catch eels for sale locally, to friends and to owners of cattle on the washes. The hives, made in Welney from osiers, had two compartments. They were baited with worms threaded on a thin piece of copper wire about 12 to 16 inches long. A small loop is made at one end of the wire and the worms are then threaded on it lengthwise. When full of worms the other end of the wire is passed through the loop and bent round it.

The bait is placed in a small hole left in the side of the first compartment and secured by a flat pliable piece of osier. Eels are attracted to the worms and in trying to get out push into the second compartment through a restricted entrance of flexible osiers through which they cannot escape.

Although I did not cut osiers for eel traps, I used to cut them for thatching pegs or spits. Alfred James, known as the "Osier King" had a considerable demand for spits at that time. For this purpose the osiers were cut every other year to give shoots of the favoured diameter.

They were used whole and not split, as was the practice in some parts of the country. Using a rod hook, each stem was cut by drawing the blade towards you, as this gave a clean cut. The spits had to be pointed at one end, measured for length and then chopped off with a clean square cut to leave an even surface for the thatcher's hand when pushing them into the stack.

10. Playing Darts

I am afraid I learned very little at school, mainly because my thoughts were always on the washes and with father's cows, rather than in the schoolroom. It was not until I started to go to the Crown during the long winter evenings that I really began to have a grasp of simple arithmetic. At first, while I played dominoes, I used to watch the men playing darts, wondering how they managed to tot up the score with such facility, and subtract it from the total needed.

The usual game was for a score of 301, the scoring to start and finish with a double. When I started to play darts, the addition and subtraction proved very difficult at first but I soon found that I could do it quite easily in my head and did not need to write everything down as some of the players did. Because of this I frequently found myself with the chalk and I was a popular player in any game as the others could leave the scoring to me. In this way, without realising it at the time, I played a lot of darts and became quite skillful at it.

When I was 14 or 15 I decided to enter the match which was held annually at Christmas. The first prize was a 25lb. turkey given by a local farmer, Mr. Bedford, and any profit which was made was given to the sickness and benefit fund.

I had a small dart board on the back of the living room door and I spent most of my spare time practising on it prior to the match. My mother must have been tired of hearing the thud of darts and said to me "Do you have to keep on and on at that?"

"Mother" I said, "I am going to the Crown to try and win that turkey for you and I must practice as much as I can."

Her reply of "Don't be so stupid, you know you can't win with all those good players up there" made me even more determined to do my best to win.

When the match night came I went to the Crown with a feeling of confidence, although I was also very nervous. Each of the 46 contestants paid one shilling entrance fee. I sat on a wooden stool watching every game until it was my turn. I won easily and at the end of the first round I thought to myself "The way everyone is playing tonight, I can win if I keep calm."

After I had won my second game easily, my initial nervousness disappeared and my confidence began to assert itself and I began to play better. In the semi-final I won my first leg with my opponent still wanting 100. I also won the second leg so I had a fairly easy match to take me into the final.

The other semi-final was won by Joe Bedford, whose father had given the turkey. I felt that I had a very large measure of support from the onlookers as they were all friends and knew very well what winning the turkey would mean to our large family.

In the final I was shaking like a leaf but nevertheless managed to win the first leg. The second I lost although I was not far behind my opponent. In the third leg Joe reached a score of 32 so a double 16 would have given him the game. He had one shot at it and missed and then it was my turn.

I wanted a double 8 and in the silence I thought I could hear my knees knocking together. The first dart chipped the wire on the outside but the second was in the centre of the double and I had won.

The whole house resounded to the deafening roar which followed. My father said "Bring up a gallon of beer" and one of the others said "I'll buy another" so everyone had a drink to celebrate my win.

I was concerned about the turkey which I knew was still alive in a pen at the back of the pub. I went out with two men who caught it and seemed to take a very long time to wring its neck. With the turkey slung over my shoulder, its head almost touching the ground, I went triumphantly back into the pub to the cheers of the gathered company.

My father usually stayed until the pub closed but that night he drank his pint and we went home together. Although I had the turkey over my shoulder I felt as if I was walking on air. I was so excited and could not get home quickly enough. I went in first and proudly held the turkey in front of mother, who was sitting in front of a blazing fire. She was lost for words but her face lit up which told me all that was necessary. This was a momentous Christmas for us all as I am sure it was the first turkey the Scott family had ever been fortunate enough to have.

After that, I spent practically every evening playing darts in the Crown. It was the custom for the loser to buy his opponent a drink and many an evening I have gone to play with no more than sixpence in my pocket. If I lost I had to buy a pint, costing four pence, for each of us so I would have to ask the landlord to put it on his slate until the end of the week. Some weeks I would have to pay him as much as three shillings when I got my wages but mostly I managed to hold my own and had very little on the slate.

Playing darts taught me about friendship and comradeship, assets which were to help me through my years as a prisoner of war. When we played we were disappointed at losing but there was always the incentive to win which added zest to the game and made good players and sportsmen of us.

When I returned home from being a prisoner of war, I found that some of my brothers had become very good darts players while I had been away. After the war, darts became so popular that leagues were formed, with teams from different pubs. My brothers and I played for various teams and between us won over 100 cups or trophies. We became well known in the Welney and Littleport area.

Towards the end of 1961, on behalf of my brothers Peter, Tom, Doug, Aubrey, Brian, Maurice, Bert and myself, I issued a challenge, "We will play a team of not more than eight, and not less than six, brothers in the whole of England at darts on a home-and-away basis."

My old friend, Kit Malkin, backed us by saying that he was willing to bet a big barrel of beer that we could beat any team of brothers.

This challenge was not met during the next two years, presumably because there was not another family with six or more darts playing members. While we still hoped to play at least six brothers, we lowered our sights to challenge any five brothers. Following this, we played teams of five from Deeping St. Nicholas, Whittlesey and Outwell and won all the matches.

We continued to meet all challenges and by the end of the darts season in the spring of 1966, had only been beaten once. It was then that Anglia Television decided to present a trophy which was to be competed for by teams of three brothers. In all, ninety teams entered and by the time that we had reached the finals we had played over sixty games.

For the finals, which were televised, Maurice, Peter and I made up the team. We beat the Andrews brothers of Boston by two legs to one and were presented with the trophy which was a mounted and inscribed beer pulling handle. This was the peak of the performance of the Scott brothers' team. Since then we have seldom played together except when we have been members of one of the league teams.

11. Warden of the Washes

During 1966, staff of the Wildfowl Trust, under the guidance of Peter Scott (now Sir Peter Scott) carried out a survey of the washes to try to assess their importance to wildfowl and other birds. It became obvious to the workers that a large number of species bred in the area, while it was wintering territory for a very considerable number of wildfowl, including species which were coming under increasing pressure as their normal wintering grounds were being reclaimed for industrial or farm use. Further, it was realised that the value of the area for birds could be greatly enhanced by the establishment of a refuge on the north side of the Welney road.

Unknown to me, the washes for which I was shepherd were the ones that had been selected for special study. Consequently it came as a great surprise when, early in 1967, I answered a knock on the door to find Sir Peter standing there. During the next half hour, after telling me that an anonymous donor had given enough money for the purchase of 100 acres, he explained how he envisaged the establishment of a refuge and how he hoped it could be developed. One of the first objectives would be to dig a lagoon, which would attract Bewick's swans and supplement their existing wintering grounds. He wanted to encourage public access, providing this could be done without disturbing the birds, and also provide facilities for research, which would add to those already available at Slimbridge.

The refuge would also supplement the existing conservation areas controlled by the Royal Society for the Protection of Birds, and the Cambridgeshire and Isle of Ely Naturalists' Trust, on the south of the Welney road.

Sir Peter asked me to become warden as he wanted somebody who understood the management of grazing on the washes, the control of water in the ditches and who also possessed a knowledge of wild life in the area. It was agreed that I should work part-time with the Trust at first and continue to shepherd for private owners in addition to running the shooting syndicate. This was an acceptable and wise decision as it left me in a position to maintain good relations with other users and shooters.

I had already had some experience of working with the R.S.P.B. in connection with the black-tailed godwit. In 1952, Mr. Cottier, a Littleport schoolmaster, had seen this rare species nesting on a wash over which I was shepherd. Very few people knew about it but I was asked to protect nests from damage by grazing cattle and was therefore involved from the beginning. The return of the black-tailed godwit as a breeding species did not become general knowledge until after Prince Philip had come to see them in 1967. I think it was during the discussion over the arrangements for this visit that Mr. Cottier suggested to Sir Peter that he should ask me to be warden of his proposed new refuge.

When I started to work full time for the Wildfowl Trust in 1968, the first task was to excavate a large lagoon, with water deep enough to be used by Bewick's. Following this, a footbridge was constructed over the Hundred Foot river to allow easy access between the warden's house and the lagoon and proposed observatory.

In the first winter only a few Bewick's came and my efforts to feed them met with little success. Whenever I appeared with a bucket full of wheat, they all flew away and it was often several hours before they returned.

The second winter I decided to change my tactics. At the time, I had a little dog called Sam which I used for rounding up the cattle and sheep. It was accustomed to being near ducks and nesting birds and was trained not to interfere with them or to chase and frighten them. Fen decoy men had a dog which was trained to run in and out of a series of reed hurdles running along the decoy pipe. When the ducks saw the dog their instinctive reaction was to swim towards it and thus were gradually enticed into the decoy trap.

It occurred to me that the swans might do the same. Before I appeared with the food, I sent Sam out and made him sit at a point about 200 yards from where I wanted to put the wheat on the edge of the lagoon. I found that as soon as he appeared the swans began to watch and swim slowly towards him. While they were thus distracted, I went quietly out, threw down the food and then called him to me.

The swans, fascinated by Sam, hardly noticed me as they followed him to where I was standing, and thus they were drawn to the food.

Eventually, they became accustomed to me so that I could go out and feed them without Sam. One day I started to call and whistle as I went out with the food and found that the swans soon began to recognise me and knew my call. From then on I had no further trouble in feeding them and can now go out without any of the wildfowl on the lagoon taking fright.

It must be remembered that these swans are completely wild and apart from the food they get at Welney or Slimbridge, they must fend for themselves. The quantity of food given to them during the winter is not very large, as it is only intended that it should help to attract them to the lagoon and build up their weight in preparation for the spring migration. For most of their winter food they forage on the washes or on farmers' fields, where their main diet is potatoes which are left when the crop is being harvested.

It is important that the Bewick's do not become too tame as this might make them vulnerable to being easily trapped or netted while on their long migratory flights to and from north Siberia. I have gone to fields where large flocks were feeding and called them but have not been able to get within 100 yards before they flew away. Clearly, they only recognise me near the observatory and lagoon.

Similarly, they soon notice a stranger at the lagoon. A television company visited the refuge one day to prepare a programme in which the current "Miss Anglia" was to feature. The producer was keen to have some shots of her feeding the swans. Against my better judgement I was persuaded to let her try. I went out first and fed in the usual way but the moment "Miss Anglia" appeared all the swans flew away.

By November, 1970 the first phase of establishing the refuge was complete and the observatory was opened to the public for the first time. Visitors soon began to flock to see the spectacle of several hundred Bewick's, either by day or by floodlight at night. It was not long before extensions had to be added to the observatory to cater for the ever-increasing number of visitors.

In these early years the Trust was gradually able to acquire over 700 acres of washes, mainly through donations.

Having established a refuge for Bewick's, the next task was to construct shallower pools which would encourage waders to visit and perhaps breed. The idea was to create pools which were overlooked by hides set in screening banks.

The River Authority and Internal Drainage Board were willing to help with planning the position of the banks and raised no objection to positioning them parallel with the Hundred Foot river but would only agree to finger extensions protruding 100 yards into the washes. This is because they do not want the water flow impeded during flood time as it is desirable to clear water from the Welney road as quickly as possible.

I was loaned a bulldozer to construct the wader pool. The water needed to be shallow and I thought a fluctuating level would be desirable. This I achieved by putting a 12 inch pipe into the Hundred Foot washes internal ditch so that when the tide was fairly high, water would flow into the pool but for much of the day the river level would be below the pipe. From the pool there is a six inch pipe into a ditch. Flow through this pipe can be regulated to lower the water level between tides, gradually exposing silty mud where waders can probe and find food. Among the birds using this pool are black-tailed godwits, ruffs and reeves, greenshank, redshank, dunlin, ring plover and curlew sandpipers.

Banks have now been constructed for a quarter of a mile on either side of the observatory and will be further extended when the opportunity arises. "Fingers" with banks on either side have been built into the main banks on both sides of the observatory. Throughout the length of these screening banks, small fibre-glass hides have been inserted to give facilities for viewing the waders and ducks, such as wigeon, which do not come close to the observatory.

When the washes are flooded the banks are subjected to some fairly violent wave action if there is a high wind. Such a set of circumstances occurred in 1976 ,with the result that there was considerable erosion of the sides, causing severe damage in some places. This was repaired during the following summer when the new sides were turfed rather than seeded, to give better and quicker protection.

In addition to the banks near the observatory, there is another length on the west side of the refuge, known as the Churchman banks. To try to protect these from further damage, with the help of the Conservation Corps, willows have been planted in front. Each year, before the swans arrive they are cut down to leave a stump of about two feet so that there is no obstruction of vision from the hides, while the stumps help to break any wave action. If this experiment proves successful, similar willow screens will be planted wherever possible round the other banks.

Another problem which had to be faced was how anglers could be allowed continued access to the river Delph, a favourite stretch of water for fishing, without their movement disturbing the birds. I was reluctant to build another screening bank as this would have brought more erosion and maintenance problems. Instead, I overcame it by planting a strip of willows about 30 yards wide, which I protected from grazing animals by digging a good ditch round it. Now that the willows have grown up, anglers can walk along the top of the barrier bank between the Old Bedford river and the river Delph without being seen by birds on the refuge. I like to think that the willows help to give some shelter for the north-east or easterly winds to the many anglers who continue to enjoy their sport on this river.

Since the establishment of the Welney refuge, the number of Bewick's wintering in the area has gradually increased. By 1972 there were days in January and February when over 500 swans could be seen on the lagoon but four years later over 1,000 had been seen at one time. Each year the number of whoopers is building up, although they are far less numerous than the Bewick's. Curiously, mute swans, which were quite common in the early years, are not so numerous now, probably because of competition from the whoopers who are not afraid of them and will often drive them away.

On a typical midwinter day there might also be 30-35,000 wigeon, 5,000 pintail, 5,000 mallard, 3,000 teal, 2,000 pochard and up to 3,000 other ducks such as shovellers, gadwall, gargeny, goosanders and tufted on the refuge. Cormorants were rare visitors until 1973-74 winter, when a few could be seen perching on electric wires. Now they are regular winter visitors, their number reaching 85 in one day in December, 1978.

Geese are infrequent visitors to the refuge, although 300 pinkfeet were seen flying over in November, 1972. Very small numbers of dark-bellied Brent geese, white-fronted Bean geese and pinkfeet have been seen.

During my years as warden it has been my privilege to welcome Royal and distinguished visitors to the refuge. They have all shown great interest in our efforts and have given renewed encouragement for continuing the work to me and my staff and to the many volunteers upon whom I have to rely so much in helping to keep the refuge running satisfactorily.

I was pleased to welcome, a few years ago, Robert Dougall, who visited Welney to make a programme for Nationwide. The weekend after the programme was transmitted there was a knock on my door at 9 o'clock on the Saturday morning. The visitor asked if he could speak to Robert Dougall! That day, between 9 a.m. and 6 p.m. there were 560 visitors and in the next week a total of 1,132 visitors came. These figures have, so far not been exceeded—such is the advertising value of a TV personality!

Later that year I had a visitor of another kind. As I was going over to the observatory one day during the third week in October to see whether any swans had arrived, I was alarmed to see a light aircraft flying only just a few feet above the refuge. As I knew this was well below the permitted height, I took the number which I could see quite plainly through my binoculars.

I had a shrewd suspicion that the aircraft came from the Eriswell Aero Club which is run by the USAFA from their Lakenheath base. In response to my telephone call, I was told that I had surmised correctly and that the plane was being piloted by Captain Rogie, who normally flew Phantom jets. I think the plane must have been recalled to base for in a very short time the pilot was on the 'phone, apologising and explaining that he was looking for somewhere to land without realising that he was interfering with the birds on the refuge.

He was determined to make sure that it would not happen again and promised that in the future the area would be marked as prohibited on the Aero Club maps. In addition, he said he would like to fly over the area with me so that I could see it from the air and explain to him about the refuge.

As he could not pick me up from his military base on the appointed day, he arranged to pick me up at a landing strip at Holbeach St. Johns. We flew over the refuge and the rest of the washes and later parted the best of friends. I believe he also wrote and apologised to Sir Peter Scott.

71

Further development of banking and ditching on the refuge will be possible through the generosity of Mr. J. C. Bamford who gave a digger to the Trust at the beginning of 1979. To help finance the extra work being undertaken, Bryant and May Limited have donated £10,000 to the Trust as a result of their special sales campaign with Swan Vestas matches.

My only daughter, Carolyn, spent most of her spare time helping me on the washes. By the age of nine she could drive the old ex-post office van quite competently. Whenever I needed help with the animals she was always there to assist me.

Although she was given everything that we could afford she was never satisfied for long with anything new. What she wanted most was a brother or sister.

When she was married in 1967 she was anxious to have at least two children. At present (1979) she has three sons, aged 10, 7 and 3, but to my regret none yet shows any great interest in the washes and my way of life. But these are early days and I might yet have the pleasure of seeing a grandson carrying on the family tradition.

PRINTED BY AVOCET LIMITED,
MARWICK ROAD, MARCH, CAMBS.
TELEPHONE: MARCH (03542) 2097 AND 3230